HISTORY OF

s h i t

The MIT Press

Cambridge, Massachusetts

London, England

HISTORY OF

s h i t

DOMINIQUE LAPORTE

translation by
Nadia Benabid and Rodolphe el-Khoury, with an
introduction by Rodolphe el-Khoury

A DOCUMENTS BOOK

This book was set in Filosofia Regular by Graphic Composition, Inc. and was
printed and bound in the United States of America.

Library of Congress Cataloging-in-Publication Data

Laporte, Dominique-Gilbert, 1949–1984.
[Histoire de la merde. English]
History of shit / Dominique Laporte ; translated by Nadia Benabid and
Rodolphe el-Khoury ; with an introduction by Rodolphe el-Khoury.
p.   cm.
"A Documents book."
Includes bibliographical references and index.
ISBN 0-262-12225-1 (hc : alk. paper)
1. Feces—Miscellanea.   I. Title.
GT2835.L3613   2000
394—dc21
99-046032

*To the young
Flaubert,
for the beautiful
explanation*

•

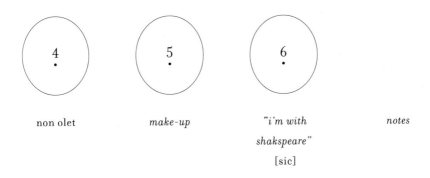

4

non olet

5

make-up

6

"i'm with
shakspeare"
[sic]

notes

introduction

Rodolphe el-Khoury

Dominique Laporte's *History of Shit* ties the concept of the individual to the fate of human waste and, in a twist that Georges Bataille would have certainly appreciated, the history of shit becomes the history of subjectivity. This conflation of the "highest" forms of consciousness with the "basest" of human products is examined in various instances of discourse and practice, language and experience. The subtitle to the French edition, "Prologue," frames the book as a beginning—a prehistory to modernity and the modern subject.

In *History of Shit*, Laporte considers the semantic atrophy of the olfactory field, a condition he relates to the Royal Academy's systematic cleansing of the French language, whose malodorous features were stifled by a thorough editing of its excremental vocabulary throughout the seventeenth century. Laporte's earlier and better-known book, *Le Français national: politique et pratiques de la langue nationale sous la Revolution Française*, co-authored with Renée Balibar, offers a detailed history of similar institutional efforts that shaped official French, focusing on the instrumental role of a streamlined and rationalized language in the construction of a centralized capitalist state.[1]

One can imagine *History of Shit* as a by-product of *Le Français national*—an aberrant discursive surplus that would have corrupted the balanced logic of that more traditional Marxist text, had it not been "laundered" by scrupulous editors. In *History of Shit*, Laporte freely indulges his scatological proclivities, drawing on the psychoanalytic frameworks of Freud and Lacan and holding Marx and Althusser at an uninhibiting arm's length.[2]

That *History of Shit* might be considered recycled waste would certainly have appealed to Laporte, given the leitmotif of the book: the return of excrement to fields of cultural production and consumption whose proper operation depends on its repression. The notion is also entirely consistent with Laporte's parody of academic discourse,[3] and with his convoluted prose, which this translation attempts to preserve; for it stands as a backhanded attempt to reverse the deodorization of language by means of a reeking syntax.

Lest anyone take his scatological fixation too seriously, Laporte states his critical ambition in quasi-Nietzschean terms: "All we can hope to do is remove a few masks with the roar of our laughter, laugh them off the figures of power." Herein lies the redeemable (and formidable) value of this excremental excursus— in its conjunction of the ridiculous with the profound, which has insights sparking with every claim of Laporte's "gay science." Readers will no doubt laugh along with the author at the outrageous claims—both reported and argued—in this book; but the speculative trajectories that Laporte engineers at such dizzying speed are no laughing matter when followed through to their grave conclusions.

Consider, for example, Laporte's reading of the Royal Edict of Villers-Cotterets from 1539, and its staggering social, cultural, and even environmental implications. The Edict decreed the private management of waste—"to each his shit." Laporte recognizes here the beginning of a formative historical process and goes on to map the construction of the "I" across private and public spheres, reconfigured in the domesticization of individual waste and odor, and with respect to institutional strategies of waste management and deodorization.

According to Freud, the decline of the olfactory sense was an inevitable outgrowth of the civilizing process, set in motion when man adopted an erect posture. From that point, he argues, "the chain of events would have proceeded through the devaluation of the olfactory stimuli and the isolation of the menstrual period to the time when visual stimuli were paramount and the genitals became visible and thence to the continuity of sexual excitation, the founding of the family and so to the threshold of civilization."[4] Laporte's *History of Shit* is consistent with Freud's general outline insofar as it recognizes the decline of the olfactory, exploits the tensions between the private nose and the public eye, and situates a historical turning point at the founding of the family.

However, the family, as conceived by Laporte, was founded in the relatively recent past. It is the social and mental construct that Annales historians have studied as a corollary to capitalist economy. The institution of a bourgeois family experience in which the odor of shit became the absolute negative reference for olfactory apprenticeship also gave rise to the individualized body and the environment that materialized its separation. Hence the consequences of Laporte's analysis are far-reaching: not only is the new olfactory economy constitutive of a bourgeois subjectivity, its effects should also be sought in the transformation of the built environment, of such things as domestic furnishing and public squares, into segregated and rationalized milieus.

In the mid-eighteenth century, Jean-François Blondel advocated a freestanding bed in accordance with the latest medical opinion on the hazards of poorly ventilated niches or alcoves. But the long historical process of the privatization of sleep had already set the ground of possibility for this architectural solution. The discomfort—moral and physical—with the promiscuity of the collective bed, manifested most tangibly in the olfactory intolerance of the odor of the other, prefigured the emergence of the individual bed, its detachment from architecture and its articulation as a discrete element in the space of the bedroom.[5]

The individual tomb is more narrowly a product of the eighteenth century and therefore more explicitly related to public health guidelines for the reorganization of urban space. Yet their logic was still largely olfactory and thus equally resonant with Laporte's analysis. Vic D'Azyr, for example, recommended a four-foot distance between separate graves in cemeteries; individuation and separation were designed to keep the "morbific rays" that emanated from the corpses from intermingling in deadly brews.[6] What quickly became an issue of personal dignity was initially sought in terms of individual odor and public promiscuity: to each his cesspool and to each his grave.

The same olfactory/excremental factors that transformed body, bed, and tomb into distinct spatial units were operative at the level of the building and the city. Their influence is clearly demonstrated in the evolution of the hospital during the second half of the eighteenth century, a process in which many recent studies have recognized the emerging physiognomy of modern space.[7] Its characteristic feature is discernible in the consistent compartmentalization and fragmentation of space into discrete components with sharp edges and clearly delineated contours.

For instance, in Jean-Baptiste Le Roy's 1777 proposal for a new Hôtel Dieu to the Académie, the wards are isolated and aligned as separate pavilions. "By means of this disposition," he argued, "each ward is like a kind of island in the wind, surrounded by a considerable volume of this fluid so that winds can carry off and renew it easily by the free access between them."[8]

A single and easy step separates architectural reforms in hospital and cemetery design from public health policies, large-scale urban interventions, and utopian schemes for ideal cities.[9] Hence Nicolas Ledoux's ideal city of Chaux, where the traditional urban organization is entirely relinquished in favor of an open and expanded field with freestanding structures. The buildings of Chaux are "independent of all adherence," surrounded by air, much like Jean-Baptiste Le Roy's "islands in the wind." Ledoux radicalized the general tendency toward looser and more permeable urban fabrics formulated in numerous eighteenth-century treatises and partially tested in the "openness" of the Place Louis XV. In *Observation sur l'architecture* (1765), for example, Marc-Antoine Laugier advocated the olfactory and acoustical advantages of larger urban blocks, which could accommodate independent houses within the ventilated and shielded space of a vast courtyard. Ledoux went even further, exploding the city into a vast territory of unobstructed expanses and atomized freestanding structures, thereby inaugurating two centuries of modernist town planning and suburban sprawl.

The cascading logic—which allows the water closet to flow so effortlessly into modern suburbia—accounts for the power and shock value of this book. The line of reasoning I extended from the history of shit to the history of architecture and the city may be too smooth a trajectory for Laporte's irregular thoughts. Still, his theoretical leaps have shown to be very effective when channeled into linear and "proper" paths. Several historians, myself included, have indeed exploited Laporte's "crude" material with favorable results. Shit, Laporte tirelessly reminds us, is continually being recycled into gold. *History of Shit* yields similar riches to readers who dare to probe.

HISTORY OF

s h i t

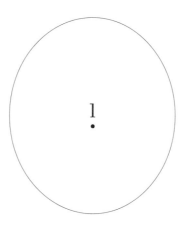

1
.

the gold of language,
the luster of scybala

Language speaks and asks:
"why am I beautiful?
Because my master bathes me."'
—Paul Éluard, *Capitale de la Douleur* (1926)

Without a master, one cannot be
cleaned. Purification, whether by fire or by the word, by baptism
or by death, requires submission to the law. It is thus, because it
has been written:

In 1539 on the 15th of August, the Day of the Assumption of
the Immaculate Virgin impregnated by the Word, the Ordinance of
Villers-Cotterets announced that henceforth justice would be ad-

ministered and civil documents and notarized acts registered in the French language:

To ensure that the significance of the aforementioned edicts is clear beyond doubt, our wish and command is that these be executed and written with a clarity that will remove all ambiguities or uncertainties which may give rise to subsequent interpretations than the ones intended.

As similar situations have often arisen in the past with regard to the significance of the Latin words contained in the aforementioned materials, we declare that henceforth all edicts, as well as other procedural documents originating in our sovereign courts as well as in subaltern or secondary institutions—be these registers, inquests, contracts, commissions, sentences, testaments, or any other and sundry acts, judicial writs, and their subsequent materials—shall be pronounced, registered, and delivered to the appropriate parties in no other than the maternal French.

In November of that same year, a second edict appeared, which until now has yet to enjoy a similar entitlement to glory. We therefore need exhume it for its substance, and in so doing, may as well abandon ourselves, albeit briefly, to the strange beauty of its language.

François, King of France by the Grace of God, makes known to all present and all to come our displeasure at the considerable deterioration visited upon our good city of Paris and its surroundings, which has in a great many places so degenerated into ruin and destruction that one cannot journey through it either by carriage or on

FIG. 1.1

horseback without meeting with great peril and inconvenience. This city and its surroundings have long endured this sorry state. Furthermore, it is so filthy and glutted with mud, animal excrement, rubble and other offals that one and all have seen fit to leave heaped before their doors, against all reason as well as against the ordinances of our predecessors, that it provokes great horror and greater displeasure in all valiant persons of substance. These scandalous and dishonorable acts are the work of corrupted individuals who sojourn and assemble in this our city and its surroundings. The corruption and stench that accompany the aforementioned muds, mucks, and other offals have been borne in times past without cause. As we consider the aforementioned situation, as it has been put before us by several people in our council, as well as other notable individuals, we find it necessary to take hasty precautions and seek appropriate remedies for the righteous governance of this our city and its surroundings, towards which we feel a singular affection as is the rightful due of the principal and most notable city of our kingdom. We have ordained, and by way of this present communication, we ordain and command the perpetual, fixed, and irrevocable implementation of the following declarations:

. . .

Article 4. —We forbid all emptying or tossing out into the streets and squares of the aforementioned city and its surroundings of refuse, offals, or putrefactions, as well as all waters whatever their nature, and we command you to delay and retain any and all stagnant and sullied waters and urines inside the confines of your homes. We enjoin you to then carry these and promptly empty them into the stream and give them chase with a bucketful of clean water to hasten their course.

. . .

Article 15. —We forbid all and any persons to leave or dispose of any manner of fodder, animal wastes, soots and ashes, mud or any other kind of unspeakable wastes on the streets. Nor may these streets be used for conflagrations or the slaughter of pigs or beasts of any kind. Indeed, we enjoin such persons to collect droppings and wastes and to gather them inside their homes, where they shall pack them into receptacles and wicker baskets to be then carried outside the afore-mentioned city and its surrounding areas.

. . .

Article 21. —We enjoin all proprietors of houses, inns, and residences not equipped with cesspools to install these immediately, in all dili-gence and without delay.

. . .

Article 23. —And to this end we wish and order that all municipal of-ficials from the various quarters and their respective subdivisions be held individually accountable to present and report in writing in the presence of our city magistrate or his lieutenant, within fifteen days of the present publication, each house in each and every quarter that is not equipped with a cesspool. In the eight subsequent days, the lords and owners of said houses, or the concierges and tenants must be informed within three months after the first injunction, which will be recorded, that they must build the aforementioned cesspools and earth closets or risk the penalty of the confiscation of their abodes, and if these abodes are churches or mortmain properties, they shall be deprived of pensions and rents ensuing from these aforementioned properties for the duration of ten years.

Article 24. —And it is our wish that, immediately after the lapse of the predetermined time, if the lords and proprietors have not met the demands of the injunction, their houses shall be handed over to us as confiscated property that shall pertain to us, without exception and with no need of additional warning, save for those mainmortes *properties which shall be seized prior to the rest.*

. . .

Article 28. —And we also forbid all butchers, meat vendors, meat roasters, bakers, small retailers as well as vendors of fowl and poultry, tavern keepers, laborers, artisans, and all manner of other persons whatever their state or condition from keeping in any area of our city or its surroundings, or having some other person keep or breed, swine, sows, pigs, goslings, pigeons, and rabbits whether these be for sale, for nourishment, for the sustenance of their households, or for any other pretext, rhyme, or reason.

Article 29. —And we enjoin all of the above, who keep or breed swine, sows, pigs, goslings, rabbits, and pigeons in the aforementioned places, to make haste and take or carry, or entrust the taking and carrying to others of all the aforementioned swine, sows, pigs, goslings, pigeons, and rabbits to be bred and fed beyond the city and its surroundings under penalty of the confiscation of those things herein named, and risk suffering corporal punishment as well; and we also enjoin all others to identify these wrongdoers and to denounce them to the law as swiftly as possible and in so doing find themselves entitled to a third part of the profits, and in failing to comply find themselves punished and subjected to an appropriate fee.

. . .

Article 31. —We wish these present ordinances published every month of the year in all the crossroads of the city of Paris and its surroundings to the accompaniment of public fanfare. They should moreover be written in large letters on parchment and suspended in the most eminent places to be found in the sixteen quarters of the aforementioned city of Paris and its surroundings, so that their content may be known and understood by all, and it will be forbidden to remove the aforementioned displays on pain of corporal punishment to be dealt by the police commissioner of each quarter.

The edict was handed down in Paris in the twenty-fifth year of grace of the reign of François I, and "thus signed by the King, Bayard, and sealed with the great green wax seal and silk ribbon."

FIG. 1.2

EX QUO APPARET LATRINAM A LAVANDO DICTAM ESSE

Besides the coincidence of their mutual ordinance in 1539, is there any reason to place these two legal texts side by side? None perhaps, except the one provided by Varron in Book II of *de Analogia*, wherein the word "latrine" is said to derive from the word *laver* [to wash] (*Ex quo apparet latrinam a lavando dictam esse*). In the end, the accuracy of Varron's etymology is hardly our true concern. Suffice to say his claim is credible; we invoke it here primarily for the light it sheds on the peculiar organization of knowledge that was the Renaissance.

THE GOLD OF LANGUAGE, THE LUSTER OF SCYBALA

If language is beautiful, it must be because a master bathes it—a master who cleans shit holes, sweeps offal, and expurgates city and speech to confer upon them order and beauty.

And what did the King's counselor advise? "What did the Roman people and their princes do," he asked, "when they were keepers of the greatest kingdom on earth and wished to expand it and make it eternal? They found no surer method than the refinement of their Latin tongue, which in the early days of their empire was rather meager and crude. Thus enriched, their language, along with the Roman law lodged therein, spread throughout their conquered realm." In such a land, where the marriage of language and law is fully consummated, its subjects will most readily adapt themselves "to French manners and mores," until "repeated use makes them all almost the same."[1]

Latin was stale. It smelled of stagnant scholasticism and musty classrooms, of esoteric and ambiguous knowledge. "We have difficulty agreeing on the significance of Latin words," said the Edict of Villers-Cotterets. A murky language for a murky city.

But is elimination sufficient? Or must one purify and polish the diamond, "root for pearls even amidst the manure of Ennius" (as another legislator of the *lingua franca* would urge two and half centuries later), wash and police the language so that none who spoke it need "fear pollute his mouth."[2]

The writer and grammarian, no less than the King, wanted language discharged. But, like the city, it had for so long held in all manner of "mud, animal excrement, grit, and other filth" that they had to climb into the gutter to clean it.

DISCHARGING THE BOOK

In his note to the reader of the *Odes*, Ronsard forewarns that he has done away with the "y," which the grammarian Meigret neglected

to "completely *blot out.*" If Ronsard chose to retain other diph-
thongs, such as "yeux," in their *"old corrupted forms* with their *unbearable stacking up* of letters that bespeak both our ignorance and
poor judgment," it is only because he was satisfied with the extent
to which he had *"discharged* his book of its burdensome load."[3]

Strictly speaking, the cleansing of language is less a political
act than an economic one. Language is liberated from excess, from
a corrupting mass that cannot be said to amount simply to the opposite of the beautiful. What the master excises is ornament: the
calligraphy that enlightens the eye; the things in language that go
beyond articulation; that which encumbers its flow and makes it
unwieldy; that which fattens language without enriching it. All
that derives from the primacy of the line and the gaze. "When writing French," says Sebilet in his *Ars Poetica,* "do not set down letters which you do not speak," those letters that "serve only to fill up
paper."

One must return to *La Deffence et illustration de la langue* F I G . 1 . 3
française, written by Joachim du Bellay in 1549, a mere ten years
after the Ordinance of Villers-Cotterets and the edict that came to
settle the score between the subject and his filth.[4] Reading *La Deffence* by way of its metaphors reveals that in both the policing of
language and the politics of shit, it is a matter of uprooting oneself
from that clinging "remnant of earth," that "Erdenrest" to which THE GOLD OF
LANGUAGE,
Goethe refers at the end of the second *Faust.*[5] We might well say THE LUSTER OF
that the poet proposes himself as the ploughman of language, the SCYBALA
cultivator who prunes language and transmutes it from "a savage
place to a domesticated one," ridding it of waste, saving it from rot,
giving it its weight in gold.

CLEAN, WELL-SPOKEN

We have known since Barthes that "when written, shit does not smell."[6] But, to ensure that readers are spared all trace of odor, language must first purge itself of a certain lingering stink. No doubt beautiful language has more than a little to do with shit, and style itself grows more precious the more exquisitely motivated by waste. Proof of this lies in the pedantry of the countless anonymous poems found even in today's latrines, or in the obscene syntactic contortions of those marginal literatures that elevate the excremental to a form of art.

And certainly the sign, as such, exercises a function of negation in relation to the real it designates. We thus readily agree with Adéodat when he writes that "filth in name is far nobler than the thing it signifies; we much prefer to hear it than to smell it."[7] Nonetheless, beautiful language cannot be reduced to the clever juxtaposition of signs that keeps things at an equal and permanent distance. A certain puritanism is needed if language is to dispel odor through syntax as well as through words.

If language was to become clean, the seventeenth century could not simply rely on "pare-fumier,"[8] which was still too redolent of the thing it signified. If "our language, once so scabrous and impolite," is to be "made elegant," cautions du Bellay, not only must it rid itself of muck and mud; its grammarians and writers must transform waste into a novel form of beauty. For du Bellay to allow himself the liberty of calling chapter 2 of *La Deffence* "That the French Language Cannot be Called Barbarian," language must already have labored to eliminate, or at least reduce, its own *barbarous* (i.e., foreign) leanings. It must already have declared its goal of self-reflexive self-sufficiency if, within the space of only a century, Vaugelas could amend "the propriety of words and phrases" to the "purity and orderliness of style,"[9] and thus regulate the practice of the well-spoken.

Cleansed, language corresponds to the three requirements of civilization declared by Freud: *cleanliness, order,* and *beauty,*[10] a definition, we might add, that has absolutely nothing to say on the subject of use. To cleanse, to order, to beautify: the fact that this discursive triad manifests itself so openly in the policing of both city and speech should give us pause. Perhaps it is not filth per se that troubles history's gaze, but the compulsion toward cleanliness that can locate its pragmatic function only after the fact.

At issue here is not whether the Edict of 1539 produced results, or if Paris, city of shit, emerged from the muck. Two and a half centuries later, Louis Sébastien Mercier painted an equally apocalyptic picture of a *polis* still mired in filth. Zola arrived on the scene long after positivist science had embraced modern hygiene as one of nature's fundamental laws. But the Paris he conjured was no less a sewer than the tenebrous city described in queasy medieval accounts.

FIG. 1.4

From the very outset, there is a manifest disproportion between punishment and crime in a royal edict that, after demanding that cesspools be built in every house, immediately confiscates those lacking them in merely three months time. "Hold on to your shit," declares the monarch. "Dispose of it only in the dark of night. Remove your pigs from sight beyond the city's walls, or I will seize your person and your goods, engulf your home in my capacious purse, and lock your body in my jail."

PORPHYRIES

There is little likelihood that these new rulings were rigorously enforced. Indeed, judging from the architecture of numerous sixteenth- and seventeenth-century castles and palaces, including Fontainebleau, Saint-Cloud, and Versailles, the King was among the first infractors of his own injunction.[11] I hardly mean to suggest that the esteem due a monarch might be diminished by finding him in a posture assumed by the commonest of mortals every day. But there is good reason to believe that an analysis of power should take seriously both the sight of a sovereign holding court on his pierced chair, and the splendor of the throne as a theater of resplendent love that splatters its subjects as they bow and kneel in pursuit of a royal turd.[12] (This ceremony, incidentally, can be understood as a lingering residue of the ancient ritual of papal coronation in which the elected pontiff was made to sit on a pierced, porphyry throne.)

CLOACA MAXIMA

Ultimately, the actual effects of the Hygiene Edict of 1539 are less significant than the fact that it introduced a *discourse* whose operations took hold, if not in other places, then at least on other fronts. However, although we can trace this discourse to an origin, we cannot make it run a teleological course; for it did little more than revive historical precedents and contributed virtually nothing to the subsequent triumph of modern hygiene.

We must therefore conclude that, where its anal constituent is concerned, civilization does not follow a rhythm of linear pro-

FIG. 1.5

gress. In *Civilization and Its Discontents* Freud may have asserted "the similitude which exists between the civilizing process and the evolution of the libido in the individual." But can this thesis really be sustained? It seems that civilization's primitive interest in excremental functions did not turn automatically into an appetite for cleanliness, order, and beauty. Otherwise, the nineteenth century's hygienic ideal would have irreversibly developed into an obsequious, meticulous, and parsimonious anality, of which our present civilization is hardly an example.

The generations of lay teachers who lovingly inspected the ears of the Republic's children refused to come to terms with civilization's drive to produce new refuse while seeking its absolute elimination. One might well see their efforts as the issuance of a form of government bent on staving off the inelegance of Flaubert's "demo*crassie.*" But the incapacity of this system to manage its own filth is lucidly betrayed by its intrepid fantasy of an elimination so complete it leaves no trace of waste.

There is something distinctly precapitalist in the inclination of the King and his poets to purify the commerce of words, to render language fluent, and to regenerate an urban circulation hindered by the accumulation of waste. This compulsive purification makes most sense when understood not as a step forward in history, but as a *regression* that paralleled the Renaissance's return to the values of antiquity in other spheres.

"Humanism," in fact, could be defined by its penchant for waste, that is, human waste. The benefits of this readily available resource were not lost on a century that revived seemingly forgotten antique customs and eagerly applied them in the cultivation of fields or the prescription of remedies, as for example in the case of *carbon humanun* which introduced "stercorary" physicians to the medical corps.[13] In rallying the Latin authors to its cultural renaissance and allying the enrichment of its language to Rome, the sixteenth century could hardly overlook that very pride of Rome, the *cloaca maxima*. If the sixteenth century did not actually revive Rome's sewer, which, in any case, could not be matched, then at least it revived the idea of the sewer.[14]

Cloaca maxima: even the most insipid history manual and the most elementary schooling in Latin seized every occasion to praise the *cloaca maxima* as the signifier of civilization par excellence, more important than concrete and sharing the aqueduct's status as the "very height of civilization" achieved by Rome. Civilization, at least according to Freud, follows a forked path. Impelled by an instinct to "subjugate the earth," it fashions socially useful values and goods. But civilization is also always driven by another aim: the gain-in-pleasure, which can never be reduced to its pragmatic dimension. *Waste* is caught in the crossroads of these "two converging goals." The necessary outcome of socially profitable production, it is the inevitable by-product of cleanliness, order, and beauty. But that which falls out of production must also be put to use; the gain-in-pleasure must be made to *enrich* civilization in a *sublimated* form. And thus we have not strayed far from the metaphors of those masters who sought to cleanse the language, from the King's poets and counselors, from De Seyssel and du Bellay.

LOSSES

What do we produce? "Organs," responds Freud, "auxiliary organs," that, being such, secrete waste. And what if the ethical, or at least aesthetic, transformations of history were understood as waste's precipitates? The sixteenth century never tired of "inventing" organs, principally those of sight; it harnessed the power of such auxiliaries as sail and prow to its motor organs to expand their field of action and extend the limits of their domain. As a result, Christopher Columbus could exclaim that "by means of gold even the doors of Paradise can be opened to the soul."[15] The sixteenth century also safeguarded against the shortcomings of scribes by stockpiling memory-traces on the printed page; the printing press produced the sediment of language.

The scribe relied on superfluity to make his task as copyist bearable, by sublimating it in calligraphy and illumination. His hand momentarily stopped its movement, tracing ceased, and the letters fell: "you shall avoid all superfluous orthographies," warns Ronsard, "and you shall place no letters in words such as cannot be pronounced; at the very least you will set them down as soberly as possible until such time as there is an improved reform." The book must be "discharged" of this "corruption" which only "fills up paper."

What happened to this discharge? What have we lost, and to what end, in the elimination of this fall of letters? Out of shit, a treasure arose: the treasure of language, of King and State.

If that which is expelled inevitably returns, we must trace its circuitous path: Shit comes back and takes the place of that which is engendered by its return, but in a transfigured, incorruptible

THE GOLD OF
LANGUAGE,
THE LUSTER OF
SCYBALA

FIGS. 1.6-7

form. Once eliminated, waste is reinscribed in the cycle of production as gold.

F I G . 1 . 8 The losses precipitated by the printing press brought the
book into the marketplace. Language's purification increased its
market share: the Edict of Villers-Cotterets did not aim to make
the French language available to all. It aimed to make of it a common currency. "To enrich, to magnify, to sublimate"—such was the
trajectory of a linguistic alchemy that shoots for gold.[16]

LANGUAGE IS A SLUT

Du Bellay, who waxes botanical in chapter three of *La Deffence*
("Why the French Language is not as Rich as Greek or Latin"),
knew full well that he had not only feminized *la langue Francoyse*,
but also based his vision of decanted language on an anal
metaphor:

16
.
17

*Hence I say of our language, it is once again blossoming without
bearing fruit, rather as a plant or sprout that has not yet flowered, let
alone put forth all the bounty of which it is capable. Certainly not
through any fault of her Nature, which is to engender along with the
best, but rather, through the laxity of her caretakers. Hence, she is
like that wild plant, condemned to the desert where it first began to
sprout without benefit of water or pruning or protection from the
brambles and thorns that have cast it into shadow, hastened its decline, and pushed it to the very brink of death. Had the ancient Romans been so neglectful of their language, it never would have grown
so rich in so short a time. But, good tillers that they were, they first
transplanted it from a savage place to a domesticated one; then, in*

order that it might bear fruit, they cut its useless branches, affixing
in their stead ones magisterially clipped from Greek. These new
branches took such hold and so came to resemble their Latin trunk
that they soon appeared not borrowed but native. From thence came
to the Latin language those flowers and fruits colored with such great
eloquence. [17]

Language comes into its own only through an act of castration that marks it as feminine. Restored to a virginal state, it dwells
in the space of the divine, the "divine order of pure bliss"[18] where
power reigns—the power of the One, the absolute Master to whom,
for example, du Bellay bows for having "made elegant . . . our language, once scabrous and impolite." Virginal, language finds itself
in the presence of the monarch who issued an edict to cleanse, to
polish, to purify. The bliss of language, of style itself, partakes of
the bliss of God. Language, according to du Bellay, is virgin and
mother; it must be watered and pruned, fattened, but not allowed
to grow old. When it fructifies, language must give birth only to itself, and the profits of its harvest must be indistinguishable from
those elements by which it is sublimated and refined.

Flowing through legal channels that were essentially equivalent to all the other languages of the kingdom through which
goods circulated, the golden language nonetheless remains a
treasure; it remains the *language of the King.* For while the elimination of waste may be a condition of beauty, the beautiful does
more than simply put itself in excrement's place. Just as the pearl
requires the mud that cultivates it, the language of the King—pure
language of virginal power—is engendered by the base languages,

THE GOLD OF
LANGUAGE,
THE LUSTER OF
SCYBALA

FIG. 1.9

waste and commerce, to which it is the equivalent. It shines even amid the base, its splendid clarity incorruptible.

FIG. 1.10Purified, language becomes the crown jewels, the site of law, of the sacred text, of translation and exchange. There, the muddied voices and their dialects are expurgated of their dross, losing their pitiful "remnants of earth" and the vile fruits of their dirty commerce. Guttersnipes and merchants cannot sully the virginal emblem of power, for the King's language does not wash them of their sins. But neither does it abandon them to their sinful state. Rather, it cleanses the fruit of their common labor, elevating it to the divine place of power freed from odor. Language and gold never traffic with traders and whores. As gold and as language, both forever deny their commerce with the base.

But "treasure not only has a brute form; it also has an aesthetic one: the accumulation of fine handiwork and chiseled jewels that come with the increase of social riches." Language too is chiseled, worked to match the transparency of the "crystal coin" in the great "social still" of circulation (Marx). Sublimated, it resembles the young girl who sells her body in exchange for the dowry that ensures virginity on her wedding night.

If the merchant was delivered from his commerce by purchasing the maidenhood, his progeny nonetheless bears the trace of tainted blood. And if commerce's dirty little business was delivered to the site of power as lustral gold, language became the golden coin that bought the silence of the King's subjects. Thus an abject and beastly insanity was transformed into the luminous, sonorous inanity that served to adorn the realm.[19]

From the golden age to the golden sun of the French monarch to the classical age, language draped herself in lamé and moved forward like a *slut*:

Gold? yellow, glittering, precious Gold?
[. . .]
Thus much of this, will make black, white; foul, fair;
Wrong, right; base, noble; old, young; coward, valiant;
[. . .] What this, you Gods? [. . .] this is it,
That makes, the wappen'd widow wed again;
[. . .] Come damned earth,
Thou common whore of mankind. [20]

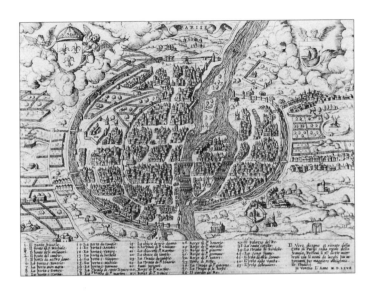

FIGURE 1.8

Shoeshine Sign in a Southern Town, 1936.

© Walker Evans Archive

The Metropolitan Museum of Art, New York.

FIGURE 1.9

Quaker steam bath, *The Shocking History of Advertising*,

E. S. Turner, Dutton Publishing, 1953.

FIGURE 1.10

Still photograph from the film *Need*, 1993.

Moyra Davey and Jason Simon.

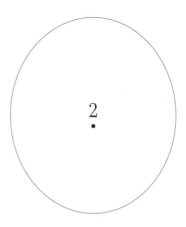

2
.

cleaning up in front of one's house,
heaping against the wall

Under the seal of divine power,
the city—site of exchange from the earliest moments of general-
ized circulation—was similarly subject to purification. Whether
belly or granary, the city is that place where merchandise accumulates and is consumed before being turned into gold. To purify the
city, one must enrich it in a manner that makes way for the means
of production. But shit cannot be converted into cash through
mere elimination. Before its restitution in sublimated form, it
must nourish the very cesspools of its production.

Undoubtedly, the city is embellished by street-sweeping, by
being "tidied"—just like the language of Vaugelas. However, repression was not the principal agent of its purification; rather,

FIG. 2.1

repression's sublimated return, through which the city was "enriched" and, at the end of the tale, came to shine with the flash of a thousand lights. Her lights would never have enlightened the world so superbly if primitive accumulation had not found in France such inspired contact with a political system bent on castration and laundering.

CLEANING UP IN FRONT OF ONE'S HOUSE

First, trash had to be sorted. "We forbid," says Article 4 of the Edict of 1539, "all emptying or tossing out into the streets and squares of the aforementioned city and its surroundings of refuse, offals, or putrefactions, as well as all waters whatever their nature, and we command you to delay and retain any and all stagnant and sullied waters and urines inside the confines of your homes. We enjoin you to then carry these and promptly empty them into the stream and give them chase with a bucketful of clean water to hasten their course." All liquids, even thick ones, must be made to circulate. Herein lies the vain aspect of waste. But let us not, in our haste, overlook the fact that where waste's vanity is concerned, the lot of urine is superior to that of stagnant waters.

The concept of matter does not delineate between solids and liquids; rather, it infiltrates liquid categories, claiming some varieties while rejecting others. If a tumbled pail of water could deliver us from waste, there would not be cause for such ado. But the situation is not so simple. Article 15 states, "we forbid all persons, whomsoever they may be, from emptying or placing any droppings, ashes, mud, or other refuse on the street, and we forbid burning on the streets and the slaughtering of swine or other beasts. We enjoin that all manner of droppings and refuse be packed into baskets or small hampers and held within the home until such time as it will be carried outside the aforementioned city and its surroundings." Article 29 amends the above by recommending that "swine, sows, pigs, birds, pigeons, and rabbits" be led outside the city altogether. Blood and shit, we realize, fare differently from parings and dishwater. But was it simply a matter of hiding waste from view, of sparing gentlefolk the sight of rustic swill? Were it simply a matter of dousing the city in a stream of clean water, there would have been no need to implement a hierarchy of waste. But when one and all are called upon to hold in and pack excrement within the confines of their homes, an altogether different set of consequences comes to light.

FIG. 2.2   First and foremost, we witness the *domestication* of waste, as a result of which the subject sees the object assigned to its "true" place; that is to say, to his home, *in domus.* If waste ensconced itself in the home, and consequently in the private sphere (a topic to which we shall return), it must certainly have played a role in the emergence of the family and familial intimacy—institutions whose relative novelty is now widely recognized. The domestication of waste must further find its rightful place in a history of the senses that will once and for all establish a plausible historicity of smell.

The privatization of waste, a process whose universality is not a historical given, made it possible for the smell of shit to be bearable within the family setting, home to the closest social ties. Just as delousing is no longer a front-stoop activity carried out in the presence of neighbors and the mixed company of all classes, the space of defecation has not always been that of interior monologue. If we are to believe travelers' accounts, certain Australian tribes customarily converse while performing their needs. Had their civilizations been predisposed to a culture of writing, they would have made eminently suitable companions for Leopold Bloom.[1]

It is apparent that socialization is regularly subverted by the politics of waste. To touch, even lightly, on the relationship of a subject to his shit, is to modify not only that subject's relationship to the totality of his body, but his very relationship to the world and to those representations that he constructs of his situation in society. The 1539 Decree, requiring that every individual or individual family hold on to personal waste before carrying it out of the city—together with the following ruling from 1536—cast the discursive genesis of modern intimacy and individuality in an altogether unprecedented light:

Every innkeeper . . . , owner, or tenant . . . , whatever his circumstance or condition may be, and without a single exception, on any street, alley or other part of this city and its outskirts, will every day at six o'clock in the morning and at consecutive three hour intervals clean in front of his house and heap his refuse against the wall,[2] *or place it in a basket or some other receptacle until such time as the garbage collectors make their rounds, or face a fine of 10 sols. Two persons in possession of a collection cart will be allocated to each neighborhood to undertake a daily round at a fixed hour with a well-sealed, sturdy, and long container . . . announced by a small attached bell. . . . , expressly for the loading of all manner of muck . . . , along with the prohibition of tossing dishwater or any other refuse from their houses . . . rather, retrieving those in baskets. . . . If the so-called muck cleansers fail to report on each and every morning and evening, they will be subjected to a fine of 100 sols . . . and even to incarceration.*[3]

FIG. 2.3

Each is bound to *"clean in front of his house."* The pronouncement is hardly a negligible step in a process already underway to individualize social practices, thereby reducing and condensing the links of contiguity to a familial space.

"Each must keep his doorstep clean": a catchy phrase, an instant proverb. Or, perhaps, a call to arms, a mobilizing and rallying *doxa*: "every man is king of his own castle"; "do not air your dirty laundry," etc. This little pile of shit, heaped here before my door, is mine, and I challenge any to malign its form. This little heap is my thing, my badge, a tangible sign of that which distinguishes me from, or likens me to, my neighbor. It is also what distinguishes him from me. His heap will never be mine. Whether he be friend or foe, this alone will allow me to recognize if we are alike: neat, clean, negligent, disgusting, or obviously rotten.

The sixteenth century was hardly an era of well-tended front gardens, of geraniums and leeks gracing doorsteps. And yet, discourse of the period—legal discourse in particular—reflects a concern with disordered promiscuity, and an ideology linking propriety to property had already begun to emerge. Mind your own business, and I will mind mine, says the individual to his neighbor. What happens in my home, in my family, my dirty laundry, and all the rest is no affair of yours. This little heap in front of my door is my business; it is mine to tend.

Mine to see to; mine to mind. Thus it was that the politics of waste branded the subject to his body, and prefigured, not so insignificantly perhaps, the Cartesian ideology of the *I*.

REPETITION, RECALL

Once waste was literally domesticated, only domestic animals were permitted in the home (with the exception of those that had been duly bled and used as food). Much like sows and piglets, scybala were escorted to their destination beyond the city's limits—where animals grazed and waste nourished the soil.

If language is a golden object surrounded by the base, the city is a jewel fed by lowly operations. In waste's initial phase of transmutation, the earth is nourished and enriched and thus bears the fruit so beneficial to the city. The city, in turn, is enriched by this metamorphosed fruit that no longer smells of earth or shit. Occasionally a poet will uncover the origin of the metamorphosis and send gold back to its "damned earth," to its hay and manure, thereby momentarily bringing the cycle to a halt.

FIG. 2.4

The sixteenth century is marked by the recollection of ancient customs buried under centuries of oblivion: the use of fecal matter to fertilize the soil, once a common practice among the Romans, is one such instance.

CLEANING UP
IN FRONT
OF ONE'S HOUSE

The utility of waste is indeed a revival. The investment of waste—in particular, human waste—with value is consistently marked by a feigned oblivion of recent practices. It is offered as a discovery, or better yet a *rediscovery*, of ancient models. When the discourse of triumphant hygiene introduced the idea of profitable waste in the nineteenth century, not a single enthusiast argued for its agricultural benefits by pointing to the fresh example of its current use in the French countryside.

Rather, they found justification for the *nec plus ultra* of agricultural technology in the diaries of travelers who had journeyed to China. This pattern of repetition and revival helps us better understand the oscillations of civilization's anal imaginary: that which occupies the site of disgust at one moment in history is not necessarily disgusting at the preceding moment or the subsequent one. There are even instances of microvariations, whereby the attitude toward waste reverses, reinstituting previous practices within the space of a few short years.

Thus it was common practice in the fifteenth century (as, in fact, it had been in ancient Rome) to use urine for the cleansing of draperies and clothes. In 1493, Parisian haberdashers, incensed by this practice, appealed to the King himself: "bonnets and other effects cleansed by means of piss are neither proper nor appropriate nor healthful to place on one's head; there lurks infection in these methods."[4] But fifty years later, around 1550, this use of urine was again reintroduced.

Civilization does not distance itself unequivocally from waste but betrays its fundamental ambivalence in act after act. Traces of this ambivalence abound on the printed page. The experience of waste in sixteenth-century France was an authentic feature of its antique revival. What specifically was revived was not the Greek and Roman cult of excrement, but the intensive use of fecal matters—and above all human feces[5]—in agricultural methods practiced under the first Emperors.[6]

STERCUS HOMINI

As in the humanities, the return to antiquity in matters of waste was launched by a series of translations that coincided with the November Edict of 1539. *Opus ruralium commodorum* by Crescentius of Bologna, for example, appeared in French in 1532. This work, published for the first time in 1307, was renamed *Prouffits champestres et ruraulx,* a title that in its use of the word "profits" registers the symbolic equation of money and shit.

In 1543, Antoine Pierre introduced a translation of the truly extraordinary *Géoponica de re rustica selectorem Constantino quidem Caesari nuncupati,* a tenth-century work by the Byzantine Emperor Constantine Porphyrogenes, which Pierre entitled the *Géoponiques.* And barely ten years after the ordinance to build private cesspools, a certain Olivier de Serres asserted that the human waste collected from these new latrines made an excellent manure when mixed with other materials.[7]

All the treatises of the day concurred on the eminent status of human manure, yet they mysteriously favored pigeon droppings: "after pigeon droppings, human waste takes second place," claims the imperial author of the *Géoponiques.* We note with some amusement that in 1843 M. Darcet's pamphlet *"Latrines modèles, construites sous un colombier, ventilées au moyen de la chaleur des pigeons, et servant à la préparation de l'engrais"*[8] was published to much success. This document describes a complicated and ingenious system, whereby the rising heat generated by the pigeon coop creates a current that is funneled in a pipe through a bed of aromatic plants (lavender, sage, etc.) to emerge perfumed and wafting through the latrine's opening.

This amazing apparatus was taken entirely seriously by both its author and his contemporaries, and Darcet's widely read pamphlet was the subject of much interest. The pigeon coop's placement above the latrine proper once again illustrates the ancient preference for pigeon waste—and this in a century when chronic amnesia becomes yet again a pretext for an extended debate regarding the status of human *stercus* in the hierarchy of waste. Whether praised or condemned, every time shit erupts in human history, rehearsing the ambivalent condition of the *Erdenrest*, it is met by a militant anthropocentrism in which the love of the *stercus* as human is as exalted as the self-love of the *anthropos.* By hoisting himself to the top of the hierarchical scale of creation, especially with regard to his "excreta," man is revealed in his earthiness as eternally, hopelessly *soiled.*

SHIT, SOUL

Although the city is cleansed through the elimination of dung, human waste must be filtered through a purifying chemistry before it can enrich the earth and sprout again as gold. Waste has its alchemy as well as its medicine; each practice rests on the universally shared belief in the powers of urine and human excrement and gains particular currency in the sixteenth century when a naive agronomy grants privilege to the *stercus.*

In accordance with the prescriptions of the *Géoponiques,* human scybala can only be used for fertilizer after a lengthy process of transformation. First, waste must be allowed to lie fallow, to precipitate and decant so that its qualities will mutate from the negative pole of their origin to the positive outcome, a noble and matchless pole.

Everything is contained in everything, each thing contains FIGS. 2.5−6 both the principle and its opposite; in time, what is burned and dried up fertilizes and nourishes, rank odors turn into perfume and rot into gold. As for human dung, Constantine Porphyrogenes writes:

[I]t is recommended so as to mitigate its noxiousness to mix it with other dungs. Above all else, one should carefully ensure that plough-men not use any dung less than a year old; for, it would be of no use, not to mention the damage it might cause, given that it is such an ex-cellent source of food for beasts and snakes. Three-to-four-year-old dung is best because the passage of time will have dissipated its stench and whatever was hard in it will have softened.

This enigmatic belief can be discerned as early as the first-century writings of Columella,[9] as well as in the *Géoponiques*, which documents its currency in both the East and West. It reemerges at the beginning of the sixteenth century in the work of Crescentius of Bologna and later in the same century in agronomic treatises and Royal Ordinances. Its more recent repercussions can be found in nineteenth-century hygienic literature and its agricul- CLEANING UP IN FRONT OF ONE'S HOUSE tural applications.

The necessity of this practice implies that the body's legacy of original sin contaminates even its waste. It would seem that hu-man excrement, like the soul, carries the "noxious" trace of the body it departs. There is a *wickedness* in shit that must be given time to dissipate, or it will turn on man, burn his fields, and nourish the malevolent snake, who, after all, is the incarnation of the *Wicked One*. But if waste is decanted or purified with water, its noxious properties evaporate, leaving behind only beneficial effects.[10] Shit is not pernicious in and of itself—only through its recent association with the flesh. Only time can release its fertilizing spirit, its subtle life principle, so volatile a substance and so susceptible to transmutation.

The same spirit that infuses soil with the fecal life principle animated the sixteenth century's return to the alchemical tradition of the Middle Ages, which attributed a key role to urine in the search for the philosopher's stone. We are far from the discrimination in other epochs between good and bad excrement (between milk and shit, for example). Here, the same stercorary matter can be good or bad, positive or negative, beneficial or noxious.

When modern medicine seeks the visible signs of wholesomeness through the attentive scrutiny of excrement, it takes shape, color, and other features of feces as a tangible index of the patient's body. Jonathan Swift, who described the archaeology of that gaze, compared it to surveillance methods used by the police in their search for traces, clues, and fingerprints.

Particularly in the sixteenth and seventeenth centuries, alchemy, together with an entire sector of medical experimentation on shit, proceeded along totally different lines. Until the very eve of clinical medicine, it was maintained that shit had the potential to be unquestionably good. The *stercus* could be as much a principle of life as of death. The literal resonance of this belief is illustrated by Gryphius's work, *In latrinis mortui et occisi*, from 1593, in which the author proposes nothing less than a comprehensive census of eminent men and women who were born or died in infamous places—namely, in latrines.[11]

A life principle. It is as spirit that shit fertilizes. When, as we know from his diaries, Michelet was short on inspiration, he lingered in latrines in order to *inspire* (breathe in) the suffocating stench that awoke in him the spirit of creation.[12] Constantine Porphyrogenes, on the other hand, maintained that only when its "stench" had "evaporated," could shit (which is fire) break its pact with the devil and become nourishment and fertilizing breath.

One can speak of a politics of waste in the sixteenth century, if it is understood in terms of a slow process of repression—one that only achieves its goal in the golden age of capitalism and is hastened by socialism's reduction of man to his needs.

To this very day, civilization's ambivalence toward shit continues to be marked, on the one hand, by a will to wash those places where garbage collects (i.e., in city and speech) and, on the other, by a belief in the purifying value of waste—so long as it is human.

THE APPRENTICESHIP OF SEEING AND SMELLING

When considering the history of the senses alongside the history of modes of production and circulation, we must ask, which lights the way for the other? Through the elimination of their waste, city and speech participated in the great visual experimentation of the sixteenth and seventeenth centuries that occurred in painting; in the new astronomy, which attributed a geometric point to the eye and invented a telescope that extended the gaze to infinity; and in the primacy of the image, through which, as Barthes has demonstrated, Ignatius of Loyola established Catholic orthodoxy against the famous *auditum verbi Dei, id est fidem*,[13] which became the Protestant Reformation's rallying cry.

The city surrendered itself to sight, bowing to the demands of the gaze; it neither shocked nor corrupted the eye and even allowed itself be constituted as an image—one that edified and signified order. The ascendance of sight, however, is paralleled by the disqualification of smell. We find one repercussion of its primacy elaborated in the philosophy of Immanuel Kant: The beautiful does not smell.

As historians are well aware, a history of the senses here finds its turning point: the passage from promiscuity to modesty cannot occur without a refinement of the sense of smell that entails a lowering of the threshold of tolerance for certain odors.[14] Nonetheless, the primacy of the visible still requires the kitchen as its backdrop. That which smells muddles vision. But when withdrawn from vision, assigned to the register of the hidden, relegated to the junk room, far from simply disappearing, odor remains affirmatively inscribed in an economy of the visible. Suppression triggers a return of the repressed.

That which is banished from the town takes up residence in the country, nourishing a process of production that is known conversely as corruption. If, as rural *doxa* claims, the earth is lowly, it is not just because it makes back-breaking demands, but because it is inseparable from its vile composition. After all, *La Terre* is Zola's most persistent exhibit of shit. Nonetheless, those things expelled from the city that fatten the country eventually return in an odorless form. Take, for example, the *chrysagyre*, the tax on excrement instituted by the Emperors Vesparian and Constantine. The return of the repressed provides a framework for understanding the operation that establishes an irreducible equivalence between money and shit—the operation that renders money, so to speak, odorless. The creation and acceleration of the division between town and country—a dichotomy that enfolds the fundamental head/tail reciprocity of shit and gold—is an effect of what is thus aptly known as primitive accumulation.

The town, as opposed to the country, becomes the site of the rot-proof and advances a new space of the visible. *Where shit was, so gold shall be.* And with its entrance, gold proclaims its implicit and ambivalent relation to excrement. Beautified, ordered, aggrandized, and sublimated, the town opposes itself to the mud of the countryside. But in so doing, it also exposes itself, in the notoriously virginal face of nature, as a place of corruption. "The bourgeois reeks!" "He stinks of money!" So says the *citoyen*, fresh from the dryer of the discourse of the *Etat Vierge* and the washing machine of the Communale. If the shit that glows in the fields becomes the lasting gold of city streets, the stench of shit lingers where gold sleeps.[15]

F I G . 2 . 7

THE PURE STATE

The laws of both production and reproduction persist in subjecting the city to successive purifications, each of which betrays different nuances in the relationship of a society to its waste: from the sewers of Haussman beneath the beautiful avenues that swept through proletarian filth, to that splendid, gigantic orifice, gaping at the "belly of Paris," Les Halles. A mere two steps away from that Versailles of a Palace of Culture, its innards exposed in broad daylight like an offering of waste—decanted waste, of course—to the

CLEANING UP
IN FRONT
OF ONE'S HOUSE

gaze, the stink of its vile commerce sheltered by its proximity to Art.[16] And so, even today, power reenacts that ceremony where the despot shits in honor of his subjects, summoned to laud him for the gift of his royal turd.

FIGS. 2.8—9 Since the sixteenth century, capitalism has persistently trapped the city in the Möbius strip of a discourse whose very unity is predicated on a division that can only be dialectically related. On one side lies the rich man's discourse, which associates the poor with the vile, the vulgar, the corrupt—in other words, with shit. On the other side lies the poor man's law, which suspects corruption within luxury and wealth at the source of stench. Needless to say, both the discourse of the master and that of the slave can smell the Jew a mile away, and their olfactory sense is all the keener when it comes to the black man. If rich and poor cling to similar racist views, it is because a capitalist dynamic locks each into place as the other's filth.

Pierre Legendre superbly demonstrates how patriotic bureaucracy draws its power from a mythology of the State as "the supreme guarantor of absolute power and virginal purity, the latter being put forth as the antithesis of dirty money." Power in its naked state is revolting, as are all those things tied to a vile and earthly trade (money, blood, sex). Why do the hard links that shackle the subjects of Western institutions to a centralist power perform so flawlessly? Why do they impede all fantasies of abolishing the State and serve instead to prolong its grip? Because the State is understood as pure and inviolable, as capable of purifying the most repulsive things—even money—through the touch of its divine hand.

40
·
41

Money, therefore, is pure insofar as it belongs to the State; so are, by association, those experts who are summoned to serve it. Power, too, is pure when legitimate and divine. "Like Hercules, the State purifies all things, including the stables," writes Legendre who, following the tradition of a salvational economy that saw its finest hour in the administrative law of the French Counter Reformation, situates the State as the site of divine power, the signifier of pure order.[17] We can duly say that Gramsci's anguished investigation of the sources of State worship, which he pursued in such texts as *Notes on Machiavelli* at precisely the moment when institutionalized Marxism was indefatigably watching over the sleep of the subjects of centralism, is amply answered here. State worship is no more or less than a response to the Love that emanates from the State—that "money-shitting State" as Legendre calls it—that floods its subjects with gifts, symbolic variants on the tyrant's glorious turd, whether he be a pontiff of the Holy Roman Church or the royal pivot of a "heliotropic monarchy."[18]

In our poem, beauty is a woman who asks her male Master to wash her; none is absolved from earthly bliss without joining the castrated ranks of the celestial State, where sexual difference is sublimated in transcendental Unity. Not a female Unity, to be sure, but one inflected by a certain femininity as it approaches its Un-Sexed ideal.[19] The State, however (bourgeois by its very definition), speaks through the King, and places its law in his mouth. This latest cleansing Master is unprecedented; this is not to say that the State is born during the Renaissance, but the Modern State, which gathers the parts and parcels of a dismembered territory around a single tongue and a common currency, most certainly is. To entrench itself successfully in the exchange of goods—a circulation that achieved a dizzying momentum in the sixteenth century—the State must intervene symbolically; its economic efficiency is tightly bound up with a symbolic register. The Modern State is constituted by the *public/private* split that lies at the heart of bourgeois law. This split, it so happens, is also designed to accommodate worldly corruption—that is to say, the commerce of merchandise and flesh. The State is at once private, because of the purity of its power, and public, because of the purifying powers of its power.

Insofar as the State signifies clean money, it immediately becomes the sine qua non condition of reproduction. In theory, business dealings are conducted outside its arena, and if merchants dabble in shit, they do so from the wings of the State's stage. The State increasingly came to occupy center stage in the sixteenth and seventeenth centuries, but only because—in order to perpetuate itself and pursue the process of primitive accumulation—the site of power must distance itself from the site of shit. So as not to stall the accumulation of wealth, mercantilism must be consigned to the private sphere—not just to ensure the expansion of its activities but, more importantly, to allow for their untrammeled and autonomous development in the absence of an internal, regulating ethic.

Legendre's thoughts on this point could be developed to show that, from the fifteenth and sixteenth centuries onward, economic theory and practice are completely severed from the kinds of ethical considerations that dominate earlier eras. Never before did economy so unreservedly occupy the place of shit, the place of a corruption devoid of all moral concern. Economists have shown how the Renaissance abandoned the medieval rule of moderation-in-gain to develop mercantile theories, ranging from a primitive form of Bullionism to French industrialism and British mercantilism, all defined by the single-minded goal of enriching the Nation. We are, it seems, prone to forget that economics was not always the province of mercantilists and physiocrats: In the Middle Ages, for example, economic thought was also developed by theologians—Thomas Aquinas, Nicole Oresme, and other Fathers of the Church. Via the Doctrine of Commutative Justice and the condemnation of interest-accruing loans, canonical thought imposed an ethics of mercantile exchange and of production proper. The Modern State thus casts itself as heir to canonical thought and to the Greco-Roman tradition: It abides by a Platonic and Aristotelian division of human labor into the lowly tasks of the slave and the elevated tasks of the citizen; and it relies on Roman Law to justify its novel forms of private property and contractual freedom. It is entirely legitimate to talk of a Romano-canonical tradition of the State (especially in France), which inscribes itself in the process of production and circulation by establishing a distinction between public and private realms, through which the division between good and bad money, lustrous and whorish gold can circulate. This division permits the State to act as an alchemical still that rids the Nation's riches of all trace of corrupt dealing. It is essential that the private be absolutely and unequivocally aligned with shit. Shit can only enter the public realm as gold. This is what allows the State, as the embodiment of the public good, to rout through its citizens' waste to unearth the treasure of sedition.

AN ARCHAEOLOGY OF THE PRIVATE

Our effort to determine which of the two shapes the other—the history of the senses or economic history—does not appear to have been in vain. The politics of shit launched by the sixteenth century, which introduced the policing of waste and the privatization of excrement, demands as much. The Edict of 1539 ordered private citizens to build latrines in their homes, thereby establishing a rigorous equivalence between the terms "retreat" and "privy" to designate the place where, from then on out, nature obeys its call.

It also happens that such a policy is completely unprecedented and that privies, in the modern sense, have no historical equivalent. In the nineteenth century, a great deal of effort was made to determine whether or not the Romans benefited from what, since the sixteenth century, has been known as retreat, privy, latrine, or rest room. Not only have Roman ruins not yielded any positive proof of their existence, but architecture treatises consistently fail to mention such quarters. Exceptionally, however, in Vitruvius *Book VI*, we find the word *cellas familiaricas* (not to be readily confused with what is generally meant by *sellas familiares*). The Perrault edition of Vitruvius's work includes the following note:

Of closets. It is not easy to know for certain what Vitruvius meant by cellas familiares, sellas perforatas, ad excipienda alvi excrementa accommodats, *but* sella, *which means saddle (or stool), is altogether different from* cella, *meaning a small room. There is evidence, nonetheless, that Vitruvius did not use* cella *for* sella *inadvertently, as the subject here is the rooms that compose apartments* *and not the objects that furnish them. And we may also conclude that he has added the word* familiarica, *or* familiaris, *to designate the usage of this room dedicated to the relief of ordinary necessities. But it must be understood that what appears here as "closet" (this is how translators have rendered the words* cellas familiaricas) *was just a place to secure the chair and other furniture necessary to the room, and not the place that French designates as* le privé, *because there is no evidence of earth pits in the buildings the ancients left us. Their* latrinas *were public places to be used by those who did not have slaves to empty and wash out their basins. Their* latrinae a lavando, *according to M. Var's etymology, also speaks of the servant* quae latrinam lavat. Latrina, *as used by Plautus in this instance, can not be understood as the Roman pit, designated to be cleansed by underground canals through which the Tiber flowed. It is plausible that Plautus used the word* latrina *to say that the* Sellas familiaris *was* veluti latrina particularis.[20]*

As this passage illustrates, excremental matters were clearly subject to a public/private split in ancient Rome. But this ancient model is hardly commensurate with that of the Renaissance. If by *cellas familiarcas* we are simply to understand a place clearly circumscribed within a house where one "secures the chair and other furniture necessary to the room," then such a place would be entirely different from the *privé* stipulated by the monarchic French State. This new structure conflates the space of the *privé* with the site of *material accumulation*, a conflation further compounded by the royal injunction that all *property owners* build these so-called *private* pits "in all diligence and without delay."[21]

This language game should give us pause. In opposition to the virginal public, the *privé* is cast as the place of commerce, of notoriously dirtying business, of primitive accumulation—but it is also cast as the dejected space of domesticity. The place where one "does one's business" is also the place where waste accumulates. The hallmark of this accumulation is the individuation of waste and its assignation to the subject—legal proprietor of the product of his dejections. *To each his shit!* proclaims a new ethic of the ego decreed by a State that entitles each subject to sit his ass on his own heap of gold.

Thus, as a "private" thing—each subject's business, each proprietor's responsibility—shit becomes a political object through its constitution as the dialectical other of the "public." From the sixteenth century on, the State initiates a contradictory discourse on waste that is nonetheless consistent with its definition as a state of capitalism: a discourse that urges proprietors to become ever richer, while casting a withering eye on the foul odor of their accumulations.

The *privé*, disgusting place where one's little business is stealthily carried out while one rubs one's hands, becomes literally the place of *primitive* accumulation. It is the home of that small heap of shit which the subject tends to, maintains, even cherishes. The State, on the other hand, is the Grand Collector, the tax guzzler, the *cloaca maxima* that reigns over all that shit, channeling and purifying it, delegating a special corporation to collect it, hiding its places of business from sight. The State devises severe fines for proprietors who transgress laws ordering them to settle their affairs behind closed doors—those who, by letting the shit fly out their windows onto the street, might confirm the suspicion that "all this does not smell very good."

But, all this will not stop Trufaldin, at his window, from spilling the aromatic contents of his bedpan on Léandre,[22] nor will it stop the Duenna from ingeniously dousing Don Japhet:

FIG. 2.10

The Duenna (*opening the window*): *The night is dark.*
(*emptying a pot on Don Japhet's head*) *Watch the water!*

Don Japhet (*shouting*): *Water! Good God! Filth!*
Bad luck and bad omen.
Bad bitch, Duenna, servant or demon.
To slosh me in piss, abominable slosher.
Cascading carcass, devil's closet.

The Duenna (*again*): *Watch the water!*

Don Japhet: *That she-devil has doubled the dose.*
Horrid she-monkey! . . . Rosewater
would have been insufferable on such a frigid night,
but to be soaked thus, in her toxic spray,
when I had hoped to meet my beautiful beloved,
and now for what, I ask, in such a pungent state?
May love be damned, and balconies be damned too,
one emerges from these steeped in piss and naked.[23]

CLEANING UP
IN FRONT
OF ONE'S HOUSE

The true cleanliness of the city's streets is not at stake here. The practice of tossing one's garbage through windows continued throughout the seventeenth century. On the eve of the Revolution, it was said of Paris that "it is impossible to live in this big city without being splattered by the shovel of the garbage collector or by the foul language of the streets."[24] This only confirms that hygiene's true drive is located far from its purported aim. The goals of the waste police are directed elsewhere; and, even at the level of discourse, we cannot identify goals per se. If something like a goal can be said to be achieved, it is always at the price of a certain loss of the object (in this case, shit), which is bypassed in favor of its symbolic substitute. Furthermore, it is less the object in question that counts than the subject's relationship to it. The loss of the object enfolds a shift in the subject's relationship to his shit, a relationship that now includes his dangling and dependent position vis-a-vis the absolute State.

FIGURE 2.1

Eugène Atget, *Porte d'Asnières*, Cité Trébert, 1913.

Albumen-silver print, 7 × 9⅜".

Abbott-Levy Collection. Partial gift of

Shirley C. Burden,

The Museum of Modern Art, New York.

© 1999, The Museum of Modern Art,

New York.

FIGURE 2.2

Courtesy B. T. Batsford,

London.

FIGURE 2.3

Courtesy The Library of Congress,

Washington, D.C.

FIGURE 2.4

Seventeenth-century alchemist.

Giraudon/Art Resource,

New York.

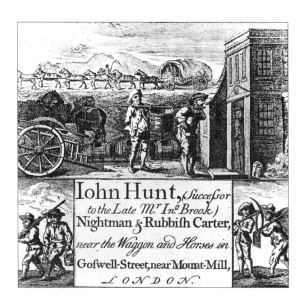

Iohn Hunt, (Succefsor
to the Late Mr Ino Brook)
Nightman & Rubbifh Carter,
near the Waggon and Horses in
Gofwell-Street, near Mount-Mill,
LONDON.

FIGURE 2.5

Francis Johnston, *Agriculture. Mixing Fertilizer.*

Hampton University's Archival and Museum Collection.

Hampton University. Hampton, Virginia.

FIGURE 2.6

Francis Johnston, *Agriculture. Plant Life. Studying the Seed.*

Hampton University's Archival and Museum Collection.

Hampton University. Hampton, Virginia.

FIGURE 2.7

"Si l'on manquait d'argent pour payer les soldats,

on leur permettait de vivre sur le peuple,"

from *Paris à Travors les A'ges* by Theodor Joseph Hoffbauer,

Firmin Didot, Paris, 1875–1882.

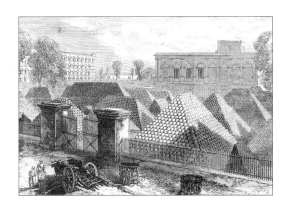

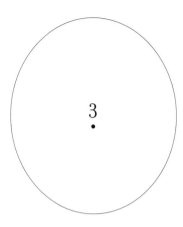

3
.

the colonial thing

Eleventh figure: the mask contorts and chews and guzzles
until it engulfs the colonial thing all is civilized curtain.

—Bernard Noël, *Le Château de Cène* (1975)

Surely, the State is the Sewer. Not
just because it spews divine law from its ravenous mouth, but because it reigns as the law of cleanliness above its sewers. Cleanliness, order, and beauty, defined by Freud as the cornerstones
of civilization, are elevated to new heights when embodied by
the State. "Civilization," says Lacan, "is the spoils: the *cloaca maxima.*"[1] We could easily substitute State here for civilization; we see
proof of this in the fact that the more it institutionalizes Freud's
triad, the more totalitarian the state becomes. Civilization is

FIG. 3.1

the opposite of what the Greeks called *barbaros* in that it is always the embodiment of pure order and divine power: the ideal, even today, of the *Etat-des-Républiques*. The proposition "civilization is the spoils" only holds if amended by a second: "the State is the Sewer."[2] Civilization is the purview of the conqueror. The barbarian craps where he pleases; the conqueror emblazons his trails with a primordial prohibition: "No shitting allowed." This injunction is retained in the memory of conquered peoples and permeates the output of their authors. In *Ulysses*, Joyce has Professor MacHugh speak out against the "foreign invaders" in the offices of the *Weekly Freeman* and the *National Press:*

The Grandeur that was Rome

—Wait a moment, Professor MacHugh said, raising two quiet claws. We mustn't be led away by words, by sounds of words. We think of Rome, imperial, imperious, imperative.

He extended elocutionary arms from frayed stained shirtcuffs, pausing:
—What was their civilization? Vast, I allow: but vile. Cloacae: *sewers. The Jews in the wilderness and on the mountaintop said: It is meet to be here. Let us build an altar to Jehovah. The Roman, like the Englishman who follows in his footsteps, brought to every new shore on which he set his foot (on our shore he never set it) only his* cloacal *obsession. He gazed about him in his toga and he said: It is meet to be here. Let us construct a water closet.*
—Which they accordingly did do, Lenehan said. Our old ancient ancestors, as we read in the first chapter of Guinness's were partial to the running stream.

—They were nature's gentlemen, J. J. O'Molloy murmured. But we have also Roman law.

—And Pontius Pilate is its prophet, Professor MacHugh responded.[3]

While business is conducted, the State looks elsewhere; it is disinclined to dirty itself with either the blood of Christ or the shit of commerce. The sole exception is Roman Law, whose subjects are purified through taxation, redeemed in exchange for their payments to the State. Pontius Pilate—that consummate Prophet of Roman Law—only became one by washing his hands in the basin of the State. Thus cleansed, he attached himself to the power of its pure order and the reign of its law that he both uttered and ushered in. This is the real reason the Christian West regards him as a stain on its memory: his act came too close to exposing power's latent image, to developing the negative of the State—the rotted reverse of the golden coin embossed with a vestal virgin. Moreover, as a ministerial representative of the conquering State, he was not in a position to administer purity. When dipping into the law, he could only bathe himself, not baptize others. (Incidentally, the truly rotten and corrupt rarely occupy the upper echelons of bureaucracy; one usually finds them stuck midway down the ladder, between the zealotry of the seconds-in-command and the all-consuming love of the censor: Pontius Pilate was a victim of centralized power.)

According to the eminent hygienist, Gaultier de Claubry, Victorian England hardly compared to Imperial Rome when it came to sewers. Clearly colored by patriotic sentiment, de Claubry's report on the matter describes those epidemics he believed to result from the circular shape of London's sewer system, which he argued led to an excessive accumulation of putrefying waste.

FIG. 3.2

Given the rage for hygiene that swept through nineteenth-century Europe, and England's role in promoting an extremely tasteful range of products that catered to new notions of cleanliness, order, and, by extension, beauty, the observations of Professor MacHugh and his acolytes could not be more *a propos*. In France, as elsewhere, a new kind of fixture would forever be attributed to its country of origin, and by the end of the nineteenth century, one only heard talk of "English basins" and "English urinals."

It seems we must take Joyce at his word when he claims a rigorous equivalence between the civilizing strategies of Imperial Rome and the British Empire. Indeed, as early as the mid-eighteenth century, Jonathan Swift anticipated what effectively became Victorian England's official line on effluvium and lucidly demonstrated the integral link between a state's imperialist tendencies and the policies of its waste police.[4]

CHARNEL HOUSES, CULT OBJECTS

To the black man, the white man looks and smells like a corpse. To the white man, the black man has the color and odor of shit. Their mutual hatred is based on a reciprocal recognition: the white man hates the black man for exposing that masked and hidden part of himself. The black man hates the white man's need to pull himself up from the earth. (The conqueror pulls himself from his native soil to till the soil of another, to exploit its capacity for production and, in so doing, cultivates it and cleanses its inhabitants.) The black man sees in the white man's need the blind arrogance of one who thinks himself immortal. But he who brings civilization cannot help but feel immortal. This is why he smells like a corpse: he is constituted by the return of that repressed "remnant of earth," which clings to him as much as to any man.

Corpses are no more and no less than waste that one buries. The Christian West has long responded with equal terror to the smell of shit and of corpses. One finds significant parallels in the morbid effects attributed to their respective odors as well as in the desire to hold them both at bay. The menace associated with the dead could only be lifted once the principle of democratic equality had been extended to dead bodies as well as to living ones. Rescued from the promiscuous anonymity of the mass grave, the corpse became the object of a cult. As an individual, the corpse ceases to be stinking offal and acquires the dignity of a relic; it severs its ties to the *cloaca* and becomes good excrement, piously preserved. Cemeteries and shit heaps find historical unity in this meeting of exquisite refuse and delicious corpses.

FIGS. 3.3—4 In the West, the tomb is a place one cultivates and decorates; that other site of embellishment for Colonial and Victorian Europe was the latrine. Both evidence a similar taste for cleanliness, for finial ornaments and fine materials. Porphyry and mahogany, porcelain and marble served as chapels to waste, and urinals sprouted on street corners like calvaries at the crossroads. Why, if not for some undisclosed kinship, did a curious mid-nineteenth century polysemy (in 1834, according to Robert and in 1836, according to Bloch and Wartburg) unite miniature chapels and urinals under the common noun, *édicule*? If, in the future, all our libraries burnt down and the field of anthropology had to be reinvented, our descendants would surely wonder what gods had been worshiped in public conveniences, their odor erased by time and their ruins as enigmatic as the ones thought today to belong to a cult of the dead.

The imperialist era effected a partial revival of the Roman FIG. 3.5 deification of human secretions, albeit in the guise of an emergent atheism. Rome, it is true, demonstrated an even greater attachment to all those things the public privy stood for in the Victorian West.[5] But the nineteenth century's compulsive cleanliness cannot adequately explain the architectural abandon with which its sites of shit were seized: these were places of commemoration. They appear almost as shrines, where civilized man deposited offerings and prayers to ward off the very awareness of his primordial origins that the revival of antique customs paradoxically invoked.

Queen Victoria may well have been a dry-fart; but this is not why Victorian London boasted the most perfect urinals and celebrated the burial of excrement in exquisite latrines. One is more likely to find the answer in the correspondence of Prince Albert, and in the particular attention he paid to human stercus. Not unlike others at the helm of Empires, he deemed it a fertilizer unmatched in quality and price, and one eminently worthy of the highest esteem—an esteem bordering on religious contemplation.

Anyone writing the history of an oppressed Ireland would certainly recognize something akin to Jonathan Swift's ferocious humor in this type of contemplation. His mock-laughter echoes a century later in the obscene grimace of Queen Victoria, collector of piss and foreskins. (Joyce, too, genially anticipates the figure of the fascist tyrant by outfitting Bello—who digs his heel in the throat of the Jew Bloom—with a mustache, green jacket, mountain climber's leggings, and plumed alpinist's hat.)

In 1726, Swift writes in his *Proposal for erecting and maintaining publick offices of ease within the cities and suburbs of London and Westminster:*

That the said [shitting] colleges be built quadrangular, with portland stone, the porticos and other ornaments in the front of marble, the statues, the basso reliefs, and sculptures of the cornishes, and the capitals of the pillars, and pilasters, being all defined to express some posture, branch, or part of evacuation; the area to be pav'd with marble, with a bason and fountain in the middle. The group of which must likewise allude to that action; a covered walk with a flat roof, supported by columns, to run around the inner quadrangle, and between every two pillars, a door to open to a shitting chamber.

That the said cells be painted in fresco, with proper grotesque figures and hieroglyphics, the seats to be covered with superfine cloth, stuff'd with cotton, and the floor, in winter time, to be overlaid with turkey carpets and in summer, strew'd with flowers and greens.[6]

It took the better part of a century for London to recognize a viable project in what had surely been conceived as caricature. It sifted fantasy from reality and built latrines minus their "appropriate grotesque frescoes." Far too often, utopias become far too real and, more often than not, they merely replicate the status quo, not to say institute new forms of out-and-out oppression. Did Swift, with his wry, grimacing humor, erect the very discourse he sought to denounce? Or were the nascent Victorian ideals of tidiness and ornamental scrolling so far advanced that the oppressed could already predict the future of his oppressor? So accurately, in fact, that he could even anticipate the space of interior monologue that Bloom conducts while unbuttoning himself to the morning air. In *Ulysses* we are told there is no difference between shitting in Ireland and shitting in London Town; both events are similarly contemplated. Hence the patriotic arrogance of Professor MacHugh: "the makers of waterclosets and the builders of sewers will never be Masters of our soul." But England, and by extension its civilization, has shown only too well that the master of waste and the warden of souls are one and the same.

THE TYRANT'S OBSCENITY

To exercise mastery over those it domesticates, the State need not delegate the inspection of privies to "philosophers and statesmen, who will be able, from the taste, smell, tincture and substance of the issue of our body's natural, to guess at the constitution of the body politic, and to inform and warn governments of all plots, design'd revolutions and intestine grumblings of restless and aspiring men."[7] The State can dispense with such lavish extremes. Its logic certainly supports the vigilant scrutiny of philosophers and statesmen. However, for the most part, the disciplinary effects of its inquisitional gaze are adequately enforced by simply removing excrement from sight.

For its subjects to participate in the body of the empire, their waste need not be subjected to microscopic scrutiny. The patrolling and controlling of orifices are sufficient strategies. It is enough to enforce a code of shitting—the master's code, the code of he who knows; namely, he who knows how to hold it in. In the long run, "sustained custom would make them all almost the same," as

De Seysell said to the king, when he called on him to follow in the footsteps of those "illustrious conquerors," the Romans, "when they were keepers of the greatest kingdom on earth and they wished to expand it and make it eternal." The task of issuing the French edition of Constanine Porphyrogenes' *Géoponica de re rustica* did not fall to the Counselor of Louis XII (although he was among the first to launch the movement of translating Ancient texts). A compulsion to make all things *almost the same* cannot fully account for the workings of a power that conflates shit and speech, and seeks to ensure the master's grip on the soul.

Is not the repetition of Sameness more effect than cause? First, the master washes himself. The cleansing of others comes later, as an aftereffect, so to speak: If I can maintain myself upright, if I can contain myself, then others must not remind me— must be prohibited from making me feel—that I once walked on all fours. Otherwise, why would the monarch deem it necessary to "sublimate" his language before enforcing its widespread use? I am beautiful because my master is pure. His purity seizes my soul with its mastery of waste. "Who is like the Lord our God? Who is seated on high? Who looks far down upon the heavens and the earth? He who raises the poor from the dust and *lifts the needy from the ash heap*, to make them sit with princes, with the princes of his people. . . ."[8] He who seizes my soul literally lifts me out of the shit. To him I swear my eternal love.

He who lifts me out of the shit will, by definition, discourage me from smelling it. He will not want me to claim that now-distanced pile—it is a repugnant thing, but one that my desperate attempts to flee only confirm as forever mine.

At times, however, in its sphincteral training of the social body, the State will invite its subjects to *smell*, much like the "obscene and ferocious" educator who punishes a child's incontinence by sticking its nose in shit, or worse.[9] Over the course of human history, the olfactory sense has been completely redefined and gains its historical momentum with the onset of the powerful State. Smell becomes the unnameable. Beautiful smell becomes an absence that arises from the elimination of odor, part and parcel of the individuation and privatization of waste.

The apprenticeship of the sense of smell directed all its efforts against the stercus. Ten years before the Edict of 1539, France imported the word for perfume, and by the second half of the 1500s (if we can take the painting of a mother wiping her child's ass as evidence), the very space of excretion was circumscribed by the family circle.[10] Distanced from his ash heap, the subject is closer to his own shit than ever before. And he can topple back into it at any moment if it pleases the all-powerful Master—he who "raises the poor from dust"—the tyrannical educator embodied in the State.

The divine right of Kings can be extended to the State insofar as it acts as a metaphor for the Lord who, *de stercore erigens pauperem*, purchases my soul with his purity. The State has the supreme power to whiten us and restore us to innocence. But the color God gives our skin plays no small part. Confronting the black race, the colonialist state faces the ultimate challenge: how to acknowledge its failure to master all things, while managing to keep its failure masked. One sees a similar rationale in the totalitarian state's conflation of blackness and irrationality in the guise of the "hysterical Negro"—that repugnant object alone capable of resisting the State's luminous seduction.[11]

FIG. 3.6

For us corpses, us colorless subjects freshly coated in the whitewash of the legitimate tyrant, the road leading from our resting place in the mass grave to the individual tomb was paved by the implementation of a discourse that disassociated shit from public display—from manure spread out in broad daylight—and relegated it to the private sphere. That moment, along with others, serves as a reference point for the inception of the modern State. When Pierre Guyotat writes, "When I admit to preferring public shit to private shit, I am simply opposing the totalitarianism of shit to the totalitarianism of the State,"[12] he reveals that one of the State's founding conditions is its application of the categories "public" and "private" to shit. The juxtaposition of a "totalitarianism of the State" and a "totalitarianism of shit" suggests that the State is no less scatophilic than its anarchic opposite. Totalitarianism simply involves (indeed, is predicated on) the relegation of shit to the private realm.

In the discourse of the State, it is a contradiction in terms to speak of "public shit." Shit ceases to be shit once it has been collected and transmuted, and only exists in the form of symbolic equivalents. To "prefer public shit to private shit" is thus to knock down the partition that separates public from private, to deny the "totalitarianism of the State" its access to the private through the construction of this dialectical division.

If the institutionalization of the septic tank marks the onset of an ease obtained at the price of a malodorous privacy, the distribution of wealth according to each person's needs marks an increasingly public and antiseptic social exchange. The subject

finds himself in the restrained posture of a force-fed goose, literally stuffed by the State that shits in his mouth.

RETENTION, THE DEATH OF THE MASTER

Spare the rod, spoil the child. The all-powerful State punishes
kulaks and other fornicators, and rewards its meritorious sons.
Ressentiment thus becomes one of the State's inevitable laws, and
the workers' revolt is transmuted into the bureaucrat's hatred of
the shopkeep. Work remains the renunciation of pleasure; but,
once rehabilitated by the State, it leads the subject to believe that
desire does not exceed need. It is understood a priori that the subject will lack for nothing. And, as the direct index of his need, his
requests to the State must fall within the bounds of reason. If a
space of pleasure remains, it is because the production of labor as
a positive object cannot take place without those saints who, in
barring the way to pleasure, reveal its potential. Much like the
blessed Saint Marie Allacoque, who consumed the excrement of
her sick charges, Lei Feng, a hero of the Cultural Revolution who
was nicknamed the "Garbage Man" because of his predilection for
the filthiest of tasks, was not viewed with distaste, but applauded
for his thoroughness and attention to a job well done. Lowering
one's buttocks into a pair of Western blue jeans is a defiling act;
cleaning up the State's filth is not. The poor man's law, which associates luxury with corruption, is here institutionalized as the
dominant discourse. Within capitalism's constitutive opposition
of the love of money and the love of purity, only that facet identified as totalitarianism persists in the myth of amply met needs.
But, generally speaking, was not the poor man better off when re-

FIG. 3.7

tention reigned, and he was trained from his tender youth to deposit his shit in a savings account? At least then he could contemplate at his leisure the Master's death and his subsequent reveling. Instead, he is condemned to fantasy: The Master is perpetually killed and the State forever murdered; but, in reality, the subject succeeds only in reinforcing the barbed wire fence. This is so much the case that, in times of peace between nations, the "inside enemy" is none other than that part of the self that must be sacrificed for the sake of the more "wholesome part" and offered up to the socialist homeland. Saving in no way anticipated this discourse, which postpones profits from its meager wealth and offers its secular label to the hereafter by promising every subject the enjoyment of riches after death.

The individuation of waste, which enjoins all "to hold and retain matter within their homes," comes attached to a moral homily; it serves as the "raw material" for a fable whose hero serves a calendar in which singing and dancing days are always a year away.

The requirement that "lords and proprietors" of Parisian houses build cesspools and retreats was not without paradox, for noblemen and bourgeoisie were not subjected to the same demand. To the aristocrat, miserliness was wretched. The compulsion to hoard was ignoble to the point of ridicule. We see this in the work of Molière, long before Balzac turned his gentlemanly gaze on the sewer and the putrefying mass of matter and merchandise where old Gobseck swims.[13] The Lords of court, those true nobles who did not have to pollute their blood by wedding the dowry of a trafficker's daughter, could continue to shit as they had before

King François's edict—in other words, without concern for waste-
fulness or expense.

It is the bourgeois who is targeted by the privatization of FIG. 3.8
waste, in the site he inhabits by definition: the city—Paris and
other like places of exchange. If he is not held accountable for
sweeping up matter or ensuring its transport outside the city, he
must nonetheless clean up before his door, under penalty of fine.[14]
And yet, if the bourgeois is targeted, it is by his own discourse.
Cleanliness has its price, or, rather, the right to be free of odor is
not without its costs. Fees, fines, and a variety of taxes serve in
turn as punishment and reward. The bourgeois redeems himself
through tithes that secure pontifical blessing, and dodges threats
worth their weight in gold.

The bourgeois is obliged to build privies and hire experts—
fyfy masters as they were called—to relieve him of his mass of filth;
or, face the looming threat of the loss of his property and, by extension, his virtual disqualification as a subject. He is forced to re-
deem himself, to escape his shameful odor, in the shelter of the
State, whose laundering treasury keeps no record of foul origins.

70
·
71

FIGURE 3.1

Sergio Vega, *Civilizacion o Barbarie*, 1998.

FIGURE 3.2

Jeremy Quennell, *The Evolution of the Water Closet*,

The Quennel Estate.

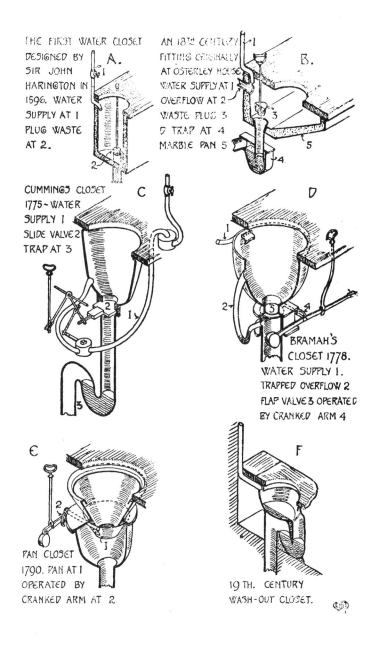

THE FIRST WATER CLOSET
DESIGNED BY
SIR JOHN
HARINGTON IN
1596. WATER
SUPPLY AT 1
PLUG WASTE
AT 2.

A.

AN 18ᵀᴴ CENTURY
FITTING ORIGINALLY
AT OSTERLEY HOUSE
WATER SUPPLY AT 1
OVERFLOW AT 2
WASTE PLUG 3
D TRAP AT 4
MARBLE PAN 5

B.

CUMMINGS CLOSET
1775 ~ WATER
SUPPLY 1
SLIDE VALVE 2
TRAP AT 3

C.

D

BRAMAH'S
CLOSET 1778.
WATER SUPPLY 1.
TRAPPED OVERFLOW 2
FLAP VALVE 3 OPERATED
BY CRANKED ARM 4

E

PAN CLOSET
1790. PAN AT 1
OPERATED BY
CRANKED ARM AT 2

F

19 TH. CENTURY
WASH-OUT CLOSET.

Joseph Bramah. Water closet. England. 1777

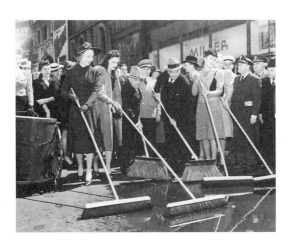

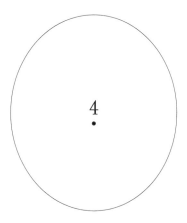

4
.

non olet

The bourgeois never reconciles himself to his "remnant of earth" and will go to great lengths to conceal it, to sneak it past even the words that name it. The eighteenth century—Voltaire, Condillac, the Physiocrats, etc., and already the end of the seventeenth century with Savary—took extreme and painstaking measures to deliver the terms "merchant" and "trader" from the disdain in which they were held. "There are Nations," wrote the Marquis de Mirabeau, "whose only attribute is trade, or what is vulgarly known as *Commerce.*" If commerce is to be an unquestionable object of love, its practitioners respected, and the specter of soiled money banished, "a civic and businessman-like spirit" must be cultivated. Thus Balzac is well justified when he writes in *Sarrasine*, "in perhaps no other country is the axiom of Vespatian better understood."

CHRYSAGIRE

According to Suetonius' legend, when Titus, son of Emperor Vespatian, blamed his father for imposing a tax on urine, Vespatian took the tax's first revenues and, placing them under his son's nose, asked if he smelt a foul odor. "Indeed not," answered Titus, who was then informed whence this gold came.[1]

The "Greatness that was Rome" had so belabored the concept of *cloaca maxima* and was so bent on cleansing the hands that its commerce soiled that, under Vespatian's rule, it went so far as to impose a tax on urine. In time, the tax was amended by Constantine to include both human and animal excrement and was christened with the quintessentially refined name *chrysagire*. Some called it "lustral gold" or "the gold of expiation." This tax was primarily levied on merchants and people of ill repute, both of whom were considered equally notorious. Beggars, whores, merchants, traders, and debtors were grouped together with dogs, donkeys, and other work animals—whose excrement was also taxed. They were grouped, in short, with the "olfactory animal," whose excessive concern with its own excrement (if one follows Freud's lead) makes it the scorn of humanity.

It is surprising that only the residue of this practice—that famous saying "Money has no smell"—has survived, since it patently states a truth that all political economies ceaselessly deny. Roman Law speaks the gospel: Where one has sinned, one will be punished. You, who have abandoned yourself to commerce, you

FIGS. 4.1–2

NON OLET

whores and dealers with your dirty hands and your reeking stench that drives away all who cross your path, you shall be made to pay in kind. Your shit itself will be taxed. Only an offering of gold, placed in the hands of the tax collector, can expiate you of your crimes. Only then shall you be washed of your sin, and what was once foul be transformed in the site of pure power. Its stench shall be lifted from it, and we shall proclaim: *non olet*. Thus the kinship of gold and shit—a complex layering of sense and sensibility, a subtle network of equivalents, synonyms and antonyms—is forged. And this kinship is rarely articulated as clearly as in Vespatian's law.

None so successfully staged this blackmail of the Educating State, this superb dialectic of punishment and redemption that keeps the subject in a state of infantile dependence, as did Constantine and Vespatian.

This is civilization at its best. Still, the subjects of Roman Law were not able to fully assent or wholeheartedly state: "Why are we so beautiful? Why is it that we, the emancipated merchants and whores, smell nothing when we gaze on ourselves in the mirror? Because our Master washes us in exchange for our shit." They may well have presented themselves every fourth year, amid cries and protestation, to set their offerings at the feet of the Great Collector, but they could never achieve complete absolution; their purity was always provisional and incidental. "Vespatian's axiom" could not entirely eradicate odor until Roman Law had been revised to accommodate the drift of growing markets. Only then could the "great social crucible" of circulation effect the transmutation whereby the origins of money are silenced in the artifice of its acquired transparency. Or, to borrow a metaphor from *Capital*, whereby money ceases to be gold and becomes crystal.

Then, and only then, could Balzac possibly write:

[T]he reserve maintained by M. and Mme. de Lanty about their origin, their past life, and their relationship with the four corners of the globe had not lasted long as a subject of astonishment in Paris. Nowhere perhaps is Vespatian's axiom better understood. There, even bloodstained or filthy money betrays nothing and stands for everything. *So long as high society knows the amount of your fortune, you are classed among those having an equal amount, and no one asks to see your family tree, because everyone knows how much it cost. In a city where social problems are solved like algebraic equations, adventurers have every opportunity in their favor. Even supposing this family were of gypsy origin, it was so wealthy, so attractive, that society had no trouble in forgiving its little secrets."*[2]

FIG. 4.3

As read by Barthes, Balzac pinpoints the transition of the use of the word "title" to describe the nobility, to its use as a claim to property—from "title deeds to ledgers." The flow of circulating goods precipitates a balanced equation that deprives the sign of its origin and extracts it from its initial referent. The cycle of blood is completed in the passage from the noble to the ignoble.[3] Henceforth, in accordance with the etiquette of the incorruptible principle of "crystal money," the bourgeois will keep silent on the subject of his birth. The ascent of the new master overturns the temporality of those who preceded his rule, makes it impossible to trace the origins of wealth, and tenaciously denies all knowledge of surplus value and primitive accumulation. Bourgeois political economy transforms origins into a tabula rasa by inventing a discourse of temporality in which it becomes possible to claim: "I was

NON OLET

never born." By elevating bodies and objects (in the form of products) to the status of signs, it places them in a translucent state; the very light that penetrates them blurs their contours, renders them opaque and tasteless, luminous and free of smell.

Much like money, bodies placed in the theater of representation no longer speak spontaneously, no longer "betray" their origins. If their mouths are sealed, they cannot say, *"inter faeces et urinas nascimur."* This is why all those things that signal shit, as such—beginning with smell—must be made to disappear. The essence of waste must be separated from shit. Once odor is gone, only matter remains.

WHAT IS PERFUME?

Of the fifty-seven procedures developed between 1762 and 1853 to disinfect cesspools, a significant number (difficult to calculate precisely, because it is often impossible to distinguish between the chemical properties of a plant and the effects of its mysterious perfume) aromatize fecal matter with bergamot, orange and lemon essence, distilled lavender, orange blossom essence, cloves, and countless other essences and oils.[4]

The workers who drained and cleaned cesspools had good reason to joke about these strange concoctions and their purported disinfecting properties: They sucked on "orange blossom–scented drops" while they worked and spoke of "shit metamorphosing into sparrows."[5] How extensively does anality deploy a metaphoric structure through which one smell is made to substitute for another? Just as in the heyday of a nascent perfume industry, manure fumes are *blocked* and a disinfection process that associates

FIG. 4.4

morbidity with odor is put into play: If bad smells cannot be eliminated, they must at least be masked by stronger and less suffocating ones.

Even today, we do not stray far from this mythology when we advertise "eau de toilette" that "make[s] your toilet water blue."[6] The putative effects of such products follow from a curious admixture of categories that blurs the lines between "tainted" (or tinted) and "disinfecting" properties. Even the most banal media advertisements still tout the myth that infection can be exorcised through the eradication of smell, or by finding ways to camouflage bad smells with good ones. In those very places where we expect to find stench, we encounter the surprising but equally strong odor of lilac or lime, lavender or pine.

Neither the lag in theory nor the noble savage's naïveté can account for the piling of the morbid atop the malodorous—and even less so for the equation of disinfection with deodorization. Since the late eighteenth century—when the 1780s ushered in a period of intense medical activity in the campaign for public health—the discourse of hygiene has been founded on such analogies. Disinfection can only ever follow the form of deodorization. This discourse appears all the more curious once we realize that alchemists, physicians, and perfume-makers had long before developed procedures to transform fecal matter into substances that not only had little or no odor, but also exhibited therapeutic qualities and the power to beautify, purify, and embellish.

NON OLET

In *The Myth of Digestion*, Bachelard points to the "digestive primitive essence" of the bourgeoisie, linking medical theories of excrement and digestion to civilization's essential anality.[7] In much the same way that a well-functioning digestive system is

FIG. 4.5

perceived as a necessary condition of good health, bad smell—whether of shit or of a corpse, from the cesspool or the cemetery—is perceived as intrinsically noxious. All unexplained pathologies are duly attributed to *mephitism* (the buzz word of nineteenth-century hygiene): repugnant exhalations that foul the air and, much like epidemics, travel from house to house spreading illness and death.

FIG. 4.6

Why should fetid odors be immediately associated with morbidity? We find at least one explanation in the myth of wholesome digestion, whereby good health is signaled by the overall absence of smells and a quasi-palatable excremental odor sets the norm. Digestion and nutrition are key factors in the transition from a blood society to a society of "health, progeny, race, survival of the species, vitality of the social body"[8]—a society where wholesome digestion (the corollary of the odorless) is likely to evince well-being. A wholesome digestion is considered beneficial to health, to the race, and to the reproduction of the species. And hence to reproduction pure and simple. Digestion is wholesome insofar as it eludes the visible and escapes the senses. It ensures and signals the sound functioning of the body by betraying none of its processes.

Translucent bodies: Wholesome digestion belongs to the economy of a society where "even bloodstained money gives away nothing and stands for everything," where the odorless (an indication, even today, of healthy shit) signals exchange and emerges as the signifier for the rich, the attractive, the beautiful. The separation of bodies from their odors guarantees the reproduction of riches, as is witnessed by hygiene's myth of "vanished excrement," whose "liquidation" (olfactory and otherwise) occurs at the very instant of its inscription in the process of production.

We are in the midst of a discourse that imitates nature in all things. Representation is thus paradoxically aligned with natural operations ("beautiful by nature"), and the sign obliges the social body to mimic nature's laws—even those for the dispersion of unpleasant odors: "nature has bestowed the entire globe with plants capable of changing mephitic air into perfume" (Bernardin de Saint-Pierre).

The triumph of the sign, of the exchangeable, is a direct accomplice of the elimination of smells, which—when not deemed pleasant or masked by a superior musk—can only be equal to their terrible selves. The concept of perfume, be it man-made or natural, is bound by the condition of odorlessness. If we speak of limits, it is because odorlessness can only be approached or approximated. Perfume, whether essence of lemon or of orange blossom, is nothing more than an inclination toward an impossible goal.

Did the cesspool workers, protected by only the false prophylactic of "orange blossom—scented drops," truly believe that the prodigies of an imagination bent on ridding shit of its smell and transforming it into "sparrows" had safeguarded them against the hazards of their profession? Or had they been forced to swallow a bitter pill that was posing as a sweet? The ideal hygienist dream quite clearly contains a compulsive need to eradicate human smell and the "olfactory animal" that man had once been. Civilization despises odor and will oust it with increased ferocity as power strives to close the gap between itself and divine purity. This ferocity reaches its peak when imperialism punishes color.

NON OLET

FIG. 4.7

Smells have no place in the constitutive triad of civilization: hygiene, order, and beauty. In the empire of hygiene and order, odor will always be suspect. Even when exquisite, it will hint at hidden filth submerged in excessive perfume, its very sweetness redolent of intoxication and vice.

THERE ARE NO BEAUTIFUL SMELLS: BEAUTY DOES NOT SMELL

Smell, the antinomy of order and hygiene, is equally incompatible with beauty.

FIG. 4.8

The European Enlightenment's political economy of the senses appears to favor the visual. The olfactory sense, at any rate, is relegated to the shadows; it is the equivalent of obscurantism. When Condillac bestows human sensation on his hypothetical statue, he starts with smell, in order to demonstrate the impoverishment of sensual experience if limited to this single crude capacity: "We thought best to begin with the sense of smell because, of all the senses, it seems to contribute least to human understanding."[9]

Condillac succeeds in demonstrating that an agreeable smell elicits pleasure and a disagreeable one pain. But this degree of discrimination (in this instance attributed to the statue who is

84
.
85

"organized internally as we are") is not enough to rehabilitate smell, to elevate its primitive status. According to Condillac, if endowed exclusively with olfaction, the statue cannot conceive of matter: It is completely overwhelmed by the object of its sensation (the statue in effect becomes smell) and is consequently incapable of entering the dimension of signification. It remains trapped in a mineral condition; at the very most, it is an animal of the lowest order ("Our statue limited to smell puts us in mind of a class of beings whose understanding is the most inferior.")[10]

Limited to the sense of smell, the statue is all smell. Without the benefit of distance, it is its own object. Smell is toppled to the lowest rung of the sensory hierarchy. Its exclusion from the realm of the intelligible is twofold. In the first place, it is excluded by definition as a sense (we are told so by Condillac twice). Second, it is seen to "contribute least to human understanding." The smelling being (statue or animal) is thus consigned to the vilest and most ignorant of states.

Excluded from epistemology, smell is no more welcome in aesthetics. The beautiful is constituted by a primordial *non olet*, which punctuates the alchemy of circulation (of both goods and signs). Fortunes have no origins; the mud behind Mme. de Lanty's attractive mask will not seep through. Once again, we find that condition already encountered in the construction of city and speech: The beautiful must not smell. This exclusion becomes definitive when its terms are commuted: "The beautiful does not smell" becomes equivalent to "There are no beautiful smells." In aesthetic discourse's repression of the excremental, the phrase assumes the latter form, especially in the work of Kant. I may say of the rose that it is beautiful, but I cannot say as much of its smell: "I describe by a judgment of taste the rose that I see as beautiful. But the judgment that results from the comparison of several singular, 'Roses in general are beautiful,' is no longer described simply as aesthetical, but as logical judgment based on an aesthetical one. Again the judgment, 'The rose is pleasant [to smell]' is,

FIG. 4.9

NON OLET

although aesthetical and singular, not a judgment of taste but of sense."[11]

Let us suppose that the rose is edible, that we judge it by its taste and not its smell; would its taste then still qualify as "good taste"? A meal can be said to be beautiful, even if the judgment has no bearing on its edibility, because food can participate in the discourse of beauty. Smell is not so fortunate; it can be good, pleasant, even exquisite, but never beautiful. Habit has sealed this exclusion. Smell resists symbolization. It obstinately clings to the index, where the materiality of its referent cannot be suppressed. Ergo: To call smell beautiful would be negligent in the extreme, since such a statement would unleash effects on beauty itself that would be impossible to contain. Were smell to be beautiful, then the beautiful would have to smell, to breathe, to sniff itself, and then what would transpire? Would not mud and blood splatter the virginal, still-translucent surface of the beautiful? Even when marvelous, smell always carries the trace of its origins.

All smells are primordially the smell of shit. This is the case, first and foremost, in providential nature: Mustiness does not ruin good smells; plants, we are told, can "change mephitic air into perfume." Perfume, *pare-fumier*, has always countered manure. By proposing itself as the counteragent of shit, perfume only ensures its persistence; denial only makes the proof more positive—shit is there. The respective pleasures of the *good* and the *beautiful* attest to this. When I say that the rose is beautiful, it is a judgment of taste. As Kant observes, "the satisfaction which determines the judgment of taste is disinterested." Conversely, the smell of the rose is not beautiful. At most, it could be called pleasant or good. "The satisfaction in the pleasant is bound up with interest," and similarly "the satisfaction in the good is bound up with interest."[12]

What is interest? It must be understood in the accountant's sense. Interest, in fact, is what motivates taste. Not any taste, naturally, but the lack of taste that is contrary to delicacy (which is itself linked to the moral and, by extension, to the beautiful and the sublime): "crude taste," "robust and hardy taste,"[13] the *commerce* of both flesh and merchandise. Such taste enlivens both facets of reproduction—the physical and the financial. This is why it is not held in absolute disdain, despite its lowly order. "As indelicate as it is, this taste cannot be scorned, for it is thanks to it that the majority of men surely and simply obey the great order of nature. It incites most marriages in the working class. It does not have its head filled with enchanting faces, languorous looks, noble bearings, etc. It understands nothing of this."[14]

Sex and money motivate this inclination, which barely qualifies as taste. "Robust, hardy, crude," it is indeed more an appetite than a sense of the beautiful. It vacillates between taste and "distaste"; at any rate, it inspires a certain dis-taste in the person of taste. Here, we find a distant residue of the "periodicity of the sexual process," when the olfactory had the upper hand and man, who had yet to raise himself from the ground, was susceptible to the "olfactory stimuli" of the menstrual cycle.[15] Smell is still entirely located in the realm of a "taste" that totters on the brink of bestiality, confined as it is by the functions of reproduction.

Even if smell cannot be beautiful, it remains at the limit that divides pleasant, good, or common taste from that which disgusts—from that which is literally the opposite of the beautiful:

"Nothing is more contrary to the beautiful than that which arouses distaste."[16]

And what, as Kant revealed long before Freud, motivates our withdrawal from the object of disgust, if not its close proximity to the beautiful? "It is concern for cleanliness that prompts us to move away from what repels. . . ."[17]

Beauty and cleanliness: Here we find two elements of the Freudian triad, conceived in the same manner as in the State's discursive attempt to partake of pure order. This discourse leads up to and includes the preceding passage from *Observations on the Feeling of the Beautiful and Sublime*, where Hume's essay "Of National Characters" inspires Kant's establishment of the irreducibility of negritude and thought, which he pronounces on behalf of white civilization's agony over the color of savage shit.

We should thus not be surprised that Kant counters the empiricist and rationalist "banishment of all beauty from the world" with an idea of natural beauty that results from chemical "precipitation." This beauty, much like the gold of alchemy, is the incorruptible precipitate of a combination of a group of pure bodies, or more specifically, of "a sudden solidification from the fluid to the solid state," that does not appear as "a mere medley of solid particles in a state of suspension."

Were odorless beauty to occur in nature, it would do so because nature functions like the "great social crucible":

Again, the watery fluids dissolved in an atmosphere that is a mixture of different gases, if they separate from the latter on account of cooling, produce no figures which, in correspondence with the special mixture of gases, often seem very artistic and are extremely beauti-

ful. So, without detracting the teleological by which we judge of organization, we may well think that the beauty of flowers, of the plumage of birds, or of shellfish, both in shape and color, may be ascribed to nature and its faculty of producing forms in an aesthetically purposive way, in its freedom, without particular purposes adapted thereto, according to chemical laws by the arrangement of the material requisite for the organization in question.[18]

FIGURE 4.4

The White Wings (training of New York city

street sweepers).

Collection of the Municipal Archives of

the City of New York.

FIGURE 4.5

Courtesy of General Electric, Inc.

FIGURE 4.6

"A dangerous water closet," *The Plumber and Sanitary Houses:*

a practical treatise on the principles of internal plumbing work, or the best

means for effectually excluding noxious gasses from our houses,

S. Steven Hellyer, 1893.

Which way would _you_ rather handle garbage?

Keep it in your kitchen ··· or

*Manufacturer's recommended retail price, including excise tax. Installation extra

WASH IT AWAY with a GE Disposall?

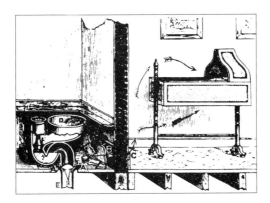

FIGURE 4.7

Eugène Atget, *Porte d'Italie, Zoniers*, 1913.

Albumen-silver print, 7 × 9⅜".

Abbott-Levy Collection. Partial gift of Shirley C. Burden,

The Museum of Modern Art, New York.

© 1999, The Museum of Modern Art, New York.

FIGURE 4.8

The nasal cavity of man showing the routes followed by inspired air.

The Scented Ape: The Biology and

Culture of Human Odour, 1990,

Michael Stoddart, Cambridge University Press.

FIGURE 4.9

Laura Larson, *Bathroom,*

Eagle's Nest, 1999.

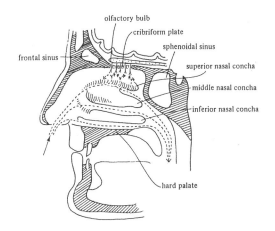

olfactory bulb

cribriform plate

frontal sinus

sphenoidal sinus

superior nasal concha

middle nasal concha

inferior nasal concha

hard palate

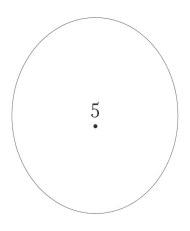

5
.

make-up

The disqualification of the olfactory ushered in a discourse whose initial outlines were furnished by the royal waste police. The sixteenth century reinvented colonization while purifying speech, and domesticated waste while promoting an aesthetic in accord with the hygienic demands of a powerful State. In so doing, it inaugurated a process that resulted in the restructuring of the hierarchy of the senses. The sense of smell was relegated to the bottom of the heap (where it will stay as long as capitalism's insatiable production considers excrement a precious commodity to be turned into gold). The new irreducibility of smell and the beautiful is also not without ties to the simultaneous emergence of a drive that extracts odor and leaves only pure matter behind.

FIGS. 5.1—2

Aesthetic's residue was production's boon: not smell, but that which smell indexes—namely, shit. Throughout the seventeenth century, the purifying, healing, and beautifying virtues of shit were sung by alchemy, medicine, chemistry, and the perfume industry. These virtues eventually receded from sight as they became less profitable. Shit lost the quasi-magical properties it had previously possessed and was reinvented as a raw material—albeit one treated with a fanaticism worthy of any prescientific myth.

As an emergent European capitalism discovered in its translations of Constantine Porphyrogenes and Crescentius of Bologna, the use of *excreta* in agricultural production had been commonplace in ancient Rome, as well as in China and Greece. The nineteenth century rediscovered the fertilizing virtues of shit by relying on ancient beliefs that saw waste (solid and liquid) as a principle of life—a remedy, a liquor, a balm, a lotion for Beauty's bath. Once its smell had been volatilized, or filtered through the aromatic plants of the Honorable Darcet's *Model Latrine built under a pigeon coop*, or submitted to any number of similar contraptions developed by his colleagues Chevalier, Fourcroy, Gaultier de Claubry, Girard, Sponi, Trèbuchet, Labarraque, Parent-Duch, Telet, etc., etc., shit became matter. It was matter, however, with spiritual powers. Shit may have served as a raw material in the capitalist ideal of production; but, in the hygienic imaginary, it remained that same primordial stuff that had so fascinated an earlier generation of alchemists and physicians.

THE STUDY OF STOMACH JUICES (*CHYOLOGIA*)

A history of the therapeutic properties of shit has yet to be written. Ideally, it would be followed by a second volume devoted to the cosmetic properties of shit, which was once used on ladies' faces and hair. There is an astounding survey to be culled from the texts of antiquity, especially those of Rome, which routinely claimed that both wounds and disease could be cured *cum stercore humano.*

Columella and Cato the Elder—notorious for their avarice—were the most prolific on the subject of human fertilizer.[1] But the works of Dioscurides, Apuleius, Catallus, Strabo (whose geography the sixteenth century took upon itself to translate), and Diodorus of Sicily all contain remarkable passages attributing the whiteness of teeth and beards, the sturdy development of once-weak children, and the recovery of sharp vision to urine.[2] Headaches were also counteracted with urine applied to the body's sensitive spots, and boiled urine ablutions were used as a prophylaxis against feminine disorders, etc.[3]

Strange correspondences arise when a learned geography of the body applies the healing powers of human waste, using it as a cooling balm for burns and a stinging cleanser for festering wounds, and concentrating its application on the antipodes (the head) and the frontal regions (the sex).

Let us now turn our attention momentarily to Pliny, whose writings provide a reasoned catalog for the uses of urine:

Our authorities attribute to urine also great power, not only natural but supernatural; they divide it into two kinds, using even that of eunuchs to counteract the sorcery that prevents fertility. But of the properties it would be proper to speak of I may mention the following:—the urine of children not yet arrived at puberty is used to counteract the spittle of the ptyas, an asp so called because it spits venom into men's eyes; for albugo, dimness, scars, argema, and affectations of the eyelids; with flour of vetch for burns; and for pus or worms in the ear if boiled down to one half with a headed leek in new earthenware. Its steam too is an emmenagogue. Salpe would foment the eyes with urine to strengthen them and would apply it for two hours at a time to a sun-burn, adding the white of an egg, by preference that of an ostrich. Urine also takes out ink blots. Men's urine relieves gout, as is shown by the testimony of fullers, who for that reason never, they say, suffer from this malady. Old urine is added to the ash of burnt oyster-shells to treat rashes on the bodies of babies, and for all running ulcers. Pitted sores, burns, affections of the anus, chaps, and scorpion stings, are treated by applications of urine. The most celebrated midwives have declared that no other lotion is better treatment for irritation of the skin, and with soda added for sores on the head, dandruff, and spreading ulcers, especially on the genitals. Each person's own urine, if it be proper for me to say so, does him the most good, if a dog-bite is immediately bathed in it, if it is applied on a sponge or wool to the quills of an urchin that are sticking in the flesh, or if ash or a serpent's bite. Moreover, for scolopendra bite a wonderful remedy is said to be for the wounded person to touch the top of his head with a drop of his own urine, when his wound is at once healed. Urine gives us symptoms of general health: if in the morning it is clear, becoming tawny later, the former means the coction is still going on, the latter that it is complete. A bad symptom is red urine, a bad one also when it bubbles, and the worst of all when it is very dark. Thick urine, in which what sinks to the bottom is *white, means that there is pain coming on about the joints or in the region of the bowels; if it is green, that the bowels are diseased. Pale urine means diseased bile, red urine diseased blood. Bad urine also is that in which is to be seen as it were bran, and cloudiness. Watery, pale urine also is unhealthy, but thick, foul-smelling urine indicates death, as does thin, watery urine from children. The Magi say that when making urine one must not expose one's person to the face of the sun or moon, or let drops fall on anyone's shadow. Hesiod advises us to urinate facing an object that screens, lest our nakedness should offend some deity. Osthanes assured people that protection against all sorcerers' potions is secured by letting one's own morning urine drip upon the foot.*[4]

Can we really claim that his beliefs are so different from our own? The color of feces still forms the basis of a no-less methodical classification of certain afflictions, complete with correspondences identically distributed on the map of the body, organized on the principle of a positive right side and sinister left one. The imagination of the ancients has been handed down to us through the centuries, at no time more forcefully than in the period between the French Renaissance and the eighteenth century. (Unless, of course, we extend our survey of the medical literature on excrement to include more recent expressions of ancient mythologies. . . .)

The *Biblioteca Scatalogica* furnishes an impressive list of works, for the most part in Latin, published between the sixteenth and the nineteenth centuries. In the sixteenth century, we find the *De excrementis*, the *De egestionibus*, and the *Dissertatio de expulsione et rententione excrementorum*; these are followed, in order of publi-

cation, by *Dissertatio de utilitate inspiciendorum ut signorum* (1693),
Dissertatio de medicina stercoraria (1700), *Chylologia historico-medica* (1725 and 1750), *Dissertatio de alvina excrementorum corporis humani coloribus variam in aegrotis significatione prebantibus*,
Swift's magestrial two-volume *Great Mystery* published in 1726,
and the comprehensive (as indicated by its title) *Dissertatio de medicamentis ex corpore humano desumptis merito negligendis*, published in 1821.

Carbon humanum, oletum, and sulfur occidentale are the most frequently mentioned treatments of stercorary medicine. But they are augmented by numerous eighteenth-century remedies compiled by Bachelard. Take, for example, *l'eau de Millefleurs*—a product made from distilled cow dung, whose efficiency varies depending on whether its source is a calf, a young cow, or a bull;[5] *Stercus nigrum*, or rat droppings, is a sure-fire remedy for constipation as well as a cure for baldness when mixed with honey and onion juices; and the shit of the *Album graecum*—an animal earth, and consequently absorbent—cures throat ailments in much the same manner as preparations of powdered ivory and knowledgeably prepared deer antlers.

Medicine's "antithetical valorization" of excrement (to borrow Bachelard's phrase) would not be so fascinating if its expression had not been systematically implicated in the aesthetic experience of shit—in other words, if, before the eighteenth century, the good and the beautiful had not been so intimately intertwined. Certainly, there are affinities between a Kantian aesthetics of shit and smell and the beliefs of both antiquity and the centuries immediately prior to the emergence of the hygienic ideal. But everything seems to indicate that those eras preceding capitalism's emergent discourse on waste were characterized more by denial than repression and were generally more willing to uphold the curative and aesthetic powers of shit—despite the existence of archaic beliefs that branded it as foul. The medical discourse on shit was simply a more developed expression of this primordial, yet ambiguous, aversion. Before Kant, one hears the refrain: "We know all too well that it stinks, and yet. . . ." Physicians, alchemists, and perfumers, bent on denying the smell of shit, placed it alongside the finest perfumes and sought to promote it—along with piss—to the rank of good object.

WHY AM I BEAUTIFUL?

Early on, medicine and its related fields placed the good and the beautiful together with the excremental. The same authors who extolled the fertilizing properties of excrement enumerated its curative powers—an equal remedy against sterility of body and soil. With similar attentiveness, they also cataloged and debated its use as a beauty product.

Who will write the history of Saint Jerome, advisor to the ladies of Rome from 382 to 385, who warned against the practice of smearing one's face with shit to preserve a youthful complexion? How could he know that the Church itself would later sanctify women who—surpassing common semen-swallowers and rivaling Sadean heroines—went so far as to ingest it? And how could Catullus, Apuleus, and Diodorus of Sicily justify their condemnation of the therapeutic practices of the Cantabrians and the Iberian Celts, who bathed and gargled with urine, when their own civilization *maxima* of the *chrysagerius* and the sewer owed the beauty of its women to the shit in which they bathed?

Taste and disgust ("dis-taste") cannot be organized along the schism of civilization and barbarity. Fifteen centuries after Longinus, young women still followed his advice and rinsed their mouths with urine to heal oral ulcers.[6] The stinging sores were appeased by fiery urine. And if love is a fire that must also be extinguished—like Pliny's lizard "who is drowned in the urine of the afflicted party to cure lovesickness"[7]—then can we not speak of the sores of love?

The history of love, shit, and the lizard also waits to be written. In ancient Egypt female hysteria was treated by making women inhale the fumes of charred crocodile dung, and the excrement of lizards was both a beauty product and a mediating element in the divine association of scarabs and shit.[8] The shit of lizards was reputed to smell like musk. So why should we be surprised that Paracelsus revived this ancient predisposition in the sixteenth century, claiming that excrement could be processed to produce the scent of musk and civet?[9] And to what should we attribute the practice, common at that time, of calling shit "civet" or "Western musk"? For the ancients, musk and shit were linked to the lizard; in later times—or at least for Paracelsus—the smell of musk was tied to human shit.

In this condensation of musk and *merde*, we once again encounter the connection—which one might be so bold to say is of the essence—between perfume and the smell of shit. The fragile boundary separating good smells from fetid ones is once again exposed. True, musk is not shit's double; but its contiguity to shit al-

FIGS. 5.3–4

MAKE-UP

lows for a displacement that is similarly cathected. Musk, we are told, is produced by a brown secretion that has an oily consistency when fresh and is hard and brittle when dry; it collects in a pouch-shaped gland of the male Asian civet, located below the abdomen and near the genital organ.[10] An entire vocabulary and set of associations have developed around this bodily topography, using the color, consistency, and fate of these secretions to support the reciprocity between musk and shit. "Native musk," for example, refers to dried cowpat. Adding yet another layer of complication to its already ambiguous status, when musk is qualified as *native* (i.e., indigenous), you can rest assured that it will stink!

Musk can be understood as the ultimate signifier, where contradictions come together and extremes collapse. This interchangeability of opposites reveals the truth of a relationship that can be only slowly unearthed. Although the odors and substances that are organized around it may be known by euphemistic appellations, musk is the site of condensation that most clearly reveals that all smell is tendentially the smell of shit. The water known as *Millefleurs* is a case in point. Its florid name notwithstanding, its status and use at the very height of the Enlightenment is nothing but a recapitulation of ancient Egypt's conviction that crocodile shit "return[ed] a wandering womb to its place."

Antiphrasis alone cannot explain how a good smell (i.e., of flowers) came to designate a product distilled from cow dung. Is there not a link between this ironic nomenclature and the derision that Parisian cesspool cleaners heaped on orange blossom-scented drops? Those workers knew full well that where there were roses, shit could not be far behind; their laughter denounced the men of science who vainly sought to deny their *Erdenrest*. The analogy between shit and perfume endures in the implicit irony of the *Mille-fleurs*—an analogy that was reiterated time and again and eventually legitimated with the seal of scientific authority:

Mr. Lemery, having purchased from his chemist half a pound of galbanum along with equal amounts of sagapenum and Judea bitumen, as well as four ounces of opopanax, and having placed all these drugs in his pockets, each wrapped in a small bag, with the exception of the sagapenum and the opopanax which were packaged together, was much surprised upon arriving at his house, to find that all present concurred that he smelled horribly of musk; each of these drugs, on its own, has an extremely unpleasant and penetrating odor, with the exception of Judea bitumen, which for its part smells nothing like musk, and all these drugs are the very ones used by medicine against vapors provoked by musk and other similar odors. He examined all the bags, one by one; they were all new, none had previously served to wrap musk, nor did they, separately, smell of musk; they smelled only of the particular prescription they had held. He assembled them together, and again, they gave off the smell of musk, the same smell which had imbued his clothing and would still be there in a rather potent form on the following day. We would not have expected these ingredients to produce a good odor.

This entry from the *Histoire de l'Académie des Sciences* (1706) serves as the pretext for perhaps the most extraordinary eighteenth-century document on the subject and uses of excrement: M. Geoffroy's *Suite de la Matière médicale*. The above anecdote, reported by a historian of the Académie, is given as proof of Paracelsus's argument that "by means of a gentle and slow digestion, it is

possible to release the smell of musk and civet from human waste."
Paracelsus adds with splendid assurance that "if human waste is
exposed to slow and repeated digestion, it can be modified in such
a way as to lose its foul odor."[11]

BECAUSE SHIT CLEANSES ME

In addition to furthering the analogy between shit and perfume,
Geoffroy's text offers one of the most beautiful examples of stercorary literature, where the beautifying power of shit is on par with
the Fountain of Youth. From it, we also learn that those very practices Saint Jerome denounced in the fourth century were still active in the eighteenth.

Numerous distillations destined for cosmetic use and an
array of beauty potions purported to whiten the skin were generated from fecal matter.[12] Its function as an elixir of youth seems
less far-fetched once we consider the host of urine-based products designed to "increase hair growth, beautify skin, improve
complexion, make scars vanish and heal chapped hands." The language that touted such miracle cures is not unlike advertising copy
today, which credits its products with secret powers to enrich and
enhance complexions and pitches them as the *precious* filtrations
of an exquisite stock.

When the *précieuse* opens her mouth, turds emerge. The *precious* fluid that pours from the priceless flask is equally artful in
masking its caustic effects; it disgorges its fire under the guise
of water and camouflages its tainted beginnings in a blaze of
metaphors. How else could the most beautiful women of their day
prize the runoff of shit and keep it on their dressing tables beside

FIG. 5.5

their most cherished fineries? And why else did they prefer the shit of the healthy, young, and pure?

The shit of athletic youths, we are told, was prized above all. In some instances, custom went so far as to exact *meconium*, the "discharge of just-born infants." In other instances, an individual was retained for the specific purpose of keeping the lady supplied. M. Geoffroy draws on the *Ephémérides d'Allemagne* (volume IX, 1752) to document the practice in his *Suite de la Matière médicale:*

[The physician] claims to have known a lady of high standing, who relied on stercorary fluid to keep her complexion the most beautiful in the world until a very advanced age. She retained a healthy young man in her service whose sole duty was to answer nature's call in a special basin of tin-plated copper equipped with a very tight lid. The deed done, the basin would immediately be covered so that none of its contents would evaporate. Once the contents had sufficiently cooled, the young man would carefully collect the moisture that had formed under the lid. This precious elixir was then poured into a flask that was kept on Madame's dressing table. Every day, without fail, this lady would wash her hands and face in the fragrant liquid; she had uncovered the secret to being beautiful for an entire lifetime. We are persuaded that this gentle and unctuous liquor can, in effect, soften and beautify the skin. But is there not extravagance in being such a slave to beauty that one wants to preserve it at all costs, even by a thing so foul and disgusting?[13]

Why should we question the authenticity of this account, when it is relayed in the spirit of dispassionate medical observation? But in the final analysis, its veracity is less important than its participation in a discursive fabric that incorporates both fiction and fact: the novels of the Marquis de Sade, for example, as well as the life of Marie Allacoque, spent happily eating the excrement of the sick to whom she tended. Beauty, it is true, did not ingest the foul liquid; she only bathed in it. But literal consumption is not required to draw a parallel between Geoffroy's account and Sade's texts. The Libertine and the Lady both kept a watchful eye on the provider of fine excrement and judged his product on the basis of its texture, color, and shape. And in both cases, a healthy young body was assigned to the task. (We can assume that the young man in question was the object of special ministrations with regard to his diet and all those other things that might have threatened his physical and general well-being.)

If special measures are only implied in the medical text, in Sade's work they are writ large. Bread, for example, "is excluded from the seraglio's menu because it would produce digestions unsuited to *coprophagia* [shit-eating]."[14] Following Barthes's reading of Sade, when the Lady chooses to bathe in her slave's shit, she (whether wittingly or unwittingly) eroticizes his turd and becomes complicit in its "elevation to the status of phallus."[15] In this give and take, Beauty, too, becomes a slave to beauty, as the good author of the *Suite médicale* sensibly remarks: The Lady would most certainly not have been blessed with the "most beautiful skin and complexion in the world" if her supply had not been furnished by a "healthy young servant." The young man's beauty is carried by his waste, as it would be by his semen, and it leaves the mark of his beauty on his Lady's cheek. This anecdote confirms, yet again, the priceless status of purified shit and the bond between purity and beauty.

OF DIVINE SHIT

When Beauty and her Roman sisters chose to disregard Saint Jerome to join the likes of Sade and Marie Allacoque, they were also upholding the traditional belief that the impure are delivered from sin by ingesting the shit of virginal clerics. In the following account from O'Donovan's *Irish Annales*, an act of bathing is transformed into an act of cleansing by way of the blessed ingestion of foul matter:

Once when he [Aedh], not yet King, came through Othna Muru, he washed his hands in the river that goes through the middle of the town. (Othna is the name of the river, and from it the town—i.e., Othna—is named.) He took a handful of water to put on his face but one of his men stopped him:

"O King," he said, "do not put that water on your face."

"Why?" asked the King.

"I am ashamed to say," he said.

"What shame can there be in speaking the truth?" asked the King.

"This is it," he replied: "the clergy's privy is over that water."

"Is it there," asked the King, "that the cleric himself goes to defecate?"

"It is indeed," said the youth.

"Not only," said the King, "shall I put it upon my face, but I shall also put it upon my mouth, and I shall drink it (drinking three mouthfuls of it), for the water into which his feces go is a sacrament to me."[16]

FIG. 5.6

MAKE-UP

We thus should not be surprised that the Christian West has been so voluble on the subject of the Eucharist—or that the stercorary has furnished the topic with its most truthful discourse. Stercorists took the words of Christ—"all things entering the mouth, descend into the stomach and leave it"—to include His body and blood. If these are instantiated by bread and wine, then they too must pass through that eventful trajectory. Indeed, King Aedh establishes the equivalence in question when he pronounces divine shit as the equal of the Eucharist. His words go a long way in explaining the sanctification of Marie Allacoque's Sadean regime as a life that is all communion.

When O'Donovan writes that "shortly after that Aedh became the king of Ireland," we understand him to mean that the legitimacy of power has its foundations in the shit of the clergy. The mouth of power swallows the shit of God himself. The shit of the holy leaves the body, yet retains its sanctity. The shit of the State drowns its subjects, yet never stops purifying them.

The most primitive beliefs run parallel to those of Church and State. The apparent kinship between the ritual of Holy Communion and numerous well-documented primitive customs involving excremental ingestion sheds a crude light on the relationship between the Church and its subjects that calls to mind the Master and his Bathed Beauty.[17] For the Namas, a Hottentot tribe, God descends "in person" (i.e., not only "in spirit") upon the shaman, who blesses marriage unions by sprinkling the betrothed with his urine.[18] Is this practice really that remote from the one Geoffroy describes? Both rely on the identity of this substance and, in both, the volatilization that subtracts odor from matter produces a discourse of the beautiful and the pure. And what of our own ritual, we civilized subjects of the Christian West, of aspersion with holy water?

Some shit is incontestably good. Not just because it has been purified, but because it is that which purifies. It purifies because it is spirit and soul—a volatilization of the flesh that retains an attachment to the body from which it has been severed. "In addition to the properties of urine, taken in and of themselves," states the *Suite de la Matière médicale*, "chemical analysis, by breaking down the active principles, also finds new remedies that are used daily to great effect; among these active principles, we find: the *spirit*, the volatile *salts*, and the *oil* of urine."[19] Shit never stops being a fragment of God. The following anecdote demonstrates this admirably—even better than the Egyptian deification of excrement or the Tibetan cult of the waste of the Great Lama (of which, incidentally, Kant was not unaware): In Polynesia, the Samoans inscribe the relationship between man and god within language by giving to every small subject the name of a divinity's shit. Once a child is conceived, a specific god is invoked, who eventually functions as a kind of "patron saint." After the child's birth, the mother asks which of the gods was called upon to protect her infant. The unnameable is named, and "out of respect for that god, the child will henceforth be known as his excrement and during his childhood is known, or 'nicknamed' 'Shit of Tongo,' or 'of Satia,' or of any other god, depending on the case."[20]

The child does not fall from on high, but is dumped as creation's refuse. Quite literally the shit of God, he finds himself doubly subject—both in body and name—to the law of *inter faeces et urinas nascimur.* Even in the most adamant atheism, shit always occupies a strange and fascinating proximity to God—from the most archaic and primitive beliefs; to the cosmic vision of the authors of the *Biblioteca Scatologica*, who asserted that "man has with good reason called a small world a microcosm, and his evacuations are but an image of those of the great world, the macrocosm"; to Brantôme's thesis, according to which we are but excrements of the earth. We dare not speak about shit. But, since the beginning of time, no other subject—not even sex—has caused us to speak so much. The unnameable is enfolded by strange rumor, which combines the most immaculate silence with the most prolix chatter. No one, not even the facetious authors of the *Biblioteca Scatalogica* (which does indeed dare to speak of shit) can escape its cosmogonic vertigo. Freud cannot, nor Bourke, whose eloquently titled book, *Scatologic Rites of all Nations,* points to the universality and timelessness of his topic.

Even discourses that lack any obvious attachment to the divine embrace a system of kinship that intimately links God, shit, and soul. And yet, despite the slumbering vigilance of militant atheism, that part of shit which is attached to an ideal of production and retained as matter remains *primitive* matter. In the end, this discourse merely serves as a springboard to a cult of materialism in which shit always comes into play as *spirit.* Indeed, its participation is marked by a spirituality tantamount to the most primitive beliefs. Despite their efforts to hide it, shit persists in the hygienist's discourse, which joins forces with philanthropy to endorse the new capitalist master. It is equally present in those related discourses from which politically instituted materialism derives. And it persists as an efficient link to the divine.

FIGURE 5.1

Postcard of Parfumerie Bruno Court,

Grasse, France, 1935.

FIGURE 5.2

Grundy Center, Iowa.

Courtesy The Library of Congress,

Washington, D.C.

FIGURE 5.3

Hans Holbein, *The Physician Visited by Death*,
Simualchres de la Mort, 1538.
(The figure of Death is holding a
sample of urine the patient has brought
to aid diagnosis.)
Select/Art Resource, New York.

You'd be proud, too!
to have a charming bathroom like this

FIGURE 5.4

Musk deer, *Perfumes and Spices*, A. H. Verrill, 1940.

General Research Division.

The New York Public Library.

Astor, Lenox and Tilden Foundations.

FIGURE 5.5

House Beautiful, May 1939.

FIGURE 5.6

Fifteenth-century latrine, *Le Decameron*,

Bibliothèque National/Bibliothèque de l'Arsenal, Paris.

MS 5070, fol. 54 v.

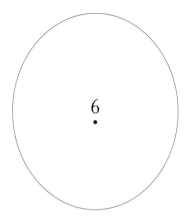

6

"i'm with shakspeare" [sic]

The most fantastical notions range around the sterile rationality of positive laws and seem, as a result, to refute ideas dear to medicine and science of yore. But the most primitive beliefs continue to be practiced quietly by those to whom capitalism has delegated the task of delivering its discourse on the body. The hygienist is a hero. He overcomes the most visceral repugnance, rolls up his shirt sleeves, and takes on the *cloaca*. He faces the foul unnameable and speaks of that thing of which no one else will speak. No one else dare name it for fear of soiling the image of his knowledge. He alone speaks of it; he alone makes it speak.

THE HYGIENIC REVOLUTION

Blood, milk, shit, sex, corpses, sperm, sewers, hospitals, facto-   FIG. 6.1
ries, urinals—for three quarters of a century, the hygienist has
spoken of these ceaselessly. He is the prince consort of bourgeois
civilization, of colonialist Europe as embodied by Queen Victoria.
Excremental issues are at the heart of his accounts, memoirs, observations, reports, letters, essays, bulletins, etc. It would be impossible to dwell on every detail; let us limit ourselves to a single
chapter in the enormous ode to cleanliness written at the beginning of the nineteenth century: It is no longer enough to eliminate
and separate shit into its solid and liquid components, to flush and
disinfect it. Now, shit has to become profitable. As Jeremy Bentham reminds us, "we never exercise, or at least should never exercise a *besoin* [in French in original text] as pure loss. It should be
put to use as manure."[1] Which is not to say that all things should be
indiscriminately made to turn a profit. Capitalism certainly profits from all things, but there are hierarchies and priorities to consider. These hierarchies can be traced back to primitive beliefs
that adhere—beyond all rational justification—to values one would
think the demands of the market would have relegated to the rank
of abandoned superstition.

It is not insignificant that the imperative of profit should be   I'M WITH
related to need [*besoin*], or that this need should be a human one.   SHAKSPEARE
[*SIC*]
The imperative of profit is not entirely driven by the imperialism
of utility, which subjugates even physiological functions. It also
marks the return of a repressed fantasy of which utility is merely
the displaced reversal, that is, the dream of satisfying all need and
thus liberating the subject from lack. Hence the primordial status

of philanthropy and hygiene alongside the supposed "three sources" in the genealogy of Marxism.[2] If a *besoin* must not be pure loss, it is because to satisfy the *besoin*, to satisfy all *besoins*, all things should serve this end, which is the corollary of the idea of need itself.

Shit as such is immediately caught in the throes of this discourse and reveals the shared stuff on which humanism and philanthropy are based. The productive value of excrement is inversely proportional to the animality of its origins. Its fertilizing powers (those of the spirit, which is in itself the life principle) are the very ones underlined in the *De Re Rustica* or the *Géoponiques:* Shit is productive only insofar as it is human. Of all the other manures known to nature, none is equal to human fertilizer.

It is hard to believe how much was written during the hygienists' movement simply to prove the superiority of human waste. The literature is truly amazing: essays by the most famous hygienists of the day; tracts by zealous physicians calling on agricultural committees to "incite serious contemplation amongst growers in a region whose agricultural fame rests on the very rational use of human secretions in their most natural state";[3] missives sent by citizens devoted to public order demanding that the prefect pay closer attention to the treatment of human waste in their region, etc. Everywhere, the virtues of human excrement were extolled, and—bedecked with the brand new prestige of the scientific method—ancient beliefs took comfort in a new legitimacy: "did not Father Shebler experimentally demonstrate that a ground sprinkled with human urine produces *twice as much* as a ground enriched by stable manure, and *almost as much* as when it is fertilized by fecal matter or the blood from slaughterhouses?"[4]

Shit owes its force, its power, its fertilizing capacity to divine prov-
idence, which places it at the summit of creation's hierarchy:

*Human fertilizer is without equal, animal fertilizers are only effec-
tive given certain conditions; they often burn harvests. Animal fertilizer has its proper place, but through a marvelously providential law,
human fertilizer has none: its place is everywhere.*[5]

Strengthened by the endorsements of learned doctors, this
pan-stercologism secularized ancient beliefs as empirical knowledge. The noxiousness that purportedly lurked in fresh excrement
was dissipated by the urgency of turning land into profit: "[T]he
practitioners counsel employing the matter in its raw or fresh
state," writes A. Sponi in his 1856 pamphlet, *Of the draining of
cesspools, in the past, present and future. Report to the magistrates of
the city of Paris.* The idea of purifying excrement was not entirely
abandoned, but distillation gave way to a canalization more in
keeping with the productive ideal and general inclinations of
Victorian Europe.

There are cases, nonetheless, when the double obsession
with sewers and profits proved antinomic. For example, article 3
of the ordinance of the police prefect of Paris, dated November 8,
1918, allowed "liquid matters to be evacuated onto the public
street when disinfected." This ruling raised a veritable hue and cry
among certain hygienists, who, on behalf of the interests of agriculture, denounced the administration for its gross negligence.
"The disinfection of cesspools," as Dr. E. L. Bertherand noted,
"poses serious problems with regard to the fertilizing properties
of excremental matter. Furthermore disinfection leads to the

I'M WITH
SHAKSPEARE
[*sic*]

FIG. 6.2

needless waste of squandered resources."[6] The hygienists accordingly developed a process for purifying excrement that would meet the demands of both public health and economic growth. Sanitation would take the form of canalization, distribution, and classification. The alchemical still of yesteryear was replaced by a relay model borrowed from methodical classifications. Disinfection, now considered in terms of divisions, first set about separating solids from liquids.

Solids are intrinsically closer to matter and, therefore, more readily able to fertilize. Liquids—owing, no doubt, to the confusion of the humid and the morbid—require more attention to ensure their separation from organic matter, from the debris of corpses, for example. This particular possibility obsessed hygienists, drawing equally on their policing instincts and their talent for scrutiny. The idea that the debris of corpses might corrupt the essence of urine merged with the suspicion that certain processes of cesspool drainage could mask all trace of the crime.[7] Hence the promotion of the sieve: To divide is to clarify.

Separators to divide liquids and solids as they funnel into the cesspool should be put in place with receptacles for the deposit, clarification and disinfection of liquids. . . . Then, and only then, will we have solved the problem, ensured health, and effected a revolution of cesspool drainage![8]

AN ARITHMETIC OF *BESOIN*

There is no doubt that these men sincerely felt they were carrying out a revolution, or that they considered themselves pioneers of a new order, willing to brave public opinion, legal authority, even personal notoriety to further their cause.

What drove them to speak so earnestly of "a revolution of cesspool drainage," to press for evacuation systems, particular modes of transport, formulas for purification? They expected nothing short of the eradication of all ills and, in the most sublime cases, the assurance of everlasting universal harmony. Essays and reports were drafted with prophetic faith. Not one of these revolutionary heroes doubted for an instant that his invention of a separator, a ventilation system, a new form of toilet bowl, or a mobile urinal would transform the future of humanity.

It is no exaggeration to say that the hygienists cherished their product. They were riveted to it, in fact, and incapable of accommodating the idea of (its) loss. Together with Bentham, they promoted a frenzied utilitarianism regarding physiological functions that can only be understood within the context of their attitude toward their own bodies—bodies inscribed in a new political economy and redefined in terms of profit and loss. The hygienist's discourse is characterized by an obvious conflation of the object that should not be lost with the reason for not losing it. It was not just that the hygienists felt responsible for the shit-money equation made famous by psychoanalysis; they were incapable of mourning the loss of the object—the loss of *their* object, more precisely. The acknowledgment of such loss could only lead to an intolerable recognition of lack—lack of sustenance, mainly. The hygienists dreamt of great harvests—of threefold, sixfold, fourteenfold yields. All this could come to pass, as long as *stercus homini* was used.

For the hygienists, shit was the site of irredeemable, even incommensurable loss, which they were obstinately bent on denying. They were caught in a tenacious thwarting of loss that sustained their delirious claim to matter, their heroic compulsion to retain. Their discourse, although synchronous with capitalism, is not the discourse of capitalism, but its symptom. Their fear of lack was not the poor man's fear. They were not likely candidates of real lack—of penury or famine. As men of means, they embodied a frugality that only later would be foisted on the people as pious.

FIGS. 6.3—4 The fear of lack not only dwells in huts; it haunts the consciousness of the bourgeoisie in the form of a primitive belief in Malthus's law of the asymmetrical relationship between the rate of a population's growth and the availability of its required resources. In the linear progression of Swiftian heterodoxy, this anxiety was assuaged by a vague belief that, in case of true need, one could always eat the children of the poor—from Ireland, or elsewhere.

Generations of schoolboys have puzzled over mathematical equations expressed in terms of spigots and intervals, bequeathed to them by the hygienists: euphemistic arithmetics that avoid naming the shameful thing. When hygienists calculated, they called shit by its name, but framed their discussion in the language of the classroom. Who will compile the marvelous mathematical formulas used by hygienists to calculate the price of shit? Take, for example, the following problem, from the brochure published in 1867 by H. Du Roselle, "Waters, Sewers, Septic Tanks, and their Relationship to Epidemics":

The fecal production of one person amounts to 750 grams per day, that is 275 kilos per year.

A family of five thus produces 1,500 kilos per year.

A farmer who would invest 10 francs in 1,000 kilos would ac-
cumulate a fortune in a short number of years.

The Proof:

100 parts of excrement of a . . .

cow	*include*	*4.1 nitrogen*
pig		*5.7* - - -
horse		*7.4* - - -
sheep		*9.1* - - -
man		*13.3* - - -

To obtain a hectare of land in fertile condition, one would
need 45,000 kilos of good manure every three years.

A farmer who cultivates 40 hectares must therefore produce
600,000 kilos of manure per year.

As a horned animal gives a maximum of 10,000 kilos of ma-
nure per year, one would therefore need 60 horned animals or horses
or the equivalent number of sheep for an area of 40 hectares.

A farmer in these conditions is rarely in possession of ¼ and
more often than not only possesses 1/10.

We harvest an average of 14 hectoliters of wheat per hectare,
which are equal to 17 or 18 francs per hectoliter, and which yield at
today's rate 350 francs per hectoliter; whereas, if we could fertilize
better, we would harvest 36 hectoliters, which would yield 900
francs.

I'M WITH
SHAKSPEARE
[*sic*]

THE OBJECT OF LOSS

How are we to understand the hygienists' efforts to demonstrate that the loss of the object would result in national disaster? How should we consider their meticulousness in keeping records, in balancing figures, and in summing up accounts? Our reckoning is further strained by the inconsistency of figures that record the volume of human waste, and the even more erratic speculations on the yields of fertilized land. Even if we multiplied the projected gains by two or by fourteen, we still could not justify the cost of shit's preservation. What is evident from this fantastic arithmetic is that the object of loss is incalculable. It is the priceless pretext that contorts arithmetic into marvelous and inconsistent figures and, in the end, demonstrates only that one cannot fix a price on the loss of shit. Dr. E. D. Bertherand, who considered cesspools and latrines from the triple perspective of "hygiene, agriculture, and commerce," introduced his communication to the Agricultural Commission with the following epigraph: "That which we lose through neglect, that which we fail to gain through ignorance, is without price."

This sentence splendidly summarizes the driving impulse of the hygienist's project: an irreparable loss that must be replenished through an excess of attention and knowledge. It is thus no accident that—when it is a matter of fulfilling *need*—the manure of choice should be human. It is only fitting that shit should be the select object of bourgeois anthropocentrism.

The objects that Freudian doctrine experiences as fundamental are here historically actualized. Shit is literally stirred up, its consequences calculated. Hygiene, as the discourse that "takes

the measure" of loss in order to overwhelm it, deserves a legitimate place within Marxism's genealogy, as, for example, when it
hails the "end of lack!"[9] To fully grasp the commonality of the
hygienic movement, philanthropy, and socialism, we must review
the work of Pierre Leroux, one of the harbingers of French socialism, whose principal writings from the 1850s coincide with the
peak of the hygienists' militant glory.

RELIGION, THE STATE, MANURE

If Pierre Leroux is still known today as a figure in the worker's
movement, his image has been purged. Rid of the smells of its beginnings, it is sent sanitized into the future, cleansed of: figures of
divine power; the subject's infantile dependence on the State; the
dream of a Golden Age, dangled by the State in its promise that
lack will be eradicated and evermore averted; pleas to master lack
and to secure the universal gratification of needs through knowledge and rational calculation. All these ideas are gathered in the
following ecstatic fragment, which exposes the blind spot of monumental bureaucracies with a truth and authenticity that is akin to
that of fiction:

FIG. 6.5

*If men were believers, experts, priests, instead of laughing as they do
at the expense of socialism, they would speak of the doctrine of the
circulus with respect and veneration. Each and every one would religiously collect their own waste and hand it over to the State, that is
to say to the tax inspector, in lieu of a tax or personal contribution.
Agricultural production would immediately double, and destitution
would disappear from the face of the earth.*

I'M WITH
SHAKSPEARE
[SIC]

FIG. 6.6 There is a great book to be had from the collected writings of Pierre Leroux. His prose may catapult us into the fictional world of Swift's *The Great Mystery*, but the preceding lines were written for the purpose of reform and published in 1850 in the first issue of *La Revue de l'Ordre social*—by no means a journal with literary aspirations. They form part of a vast corpus that includes the *Prospectus for a Agricultural Colony founded on a New Means of Subsistence*, published in 1849, as well as a highly original refutation of Malthus, entitled *Malthus and the Economists, or Will there always be poor people?* and a masterpiece of style, the astounding *Letter to the States of Jersey on the means of quintupling, at least, the country's agricultural production* (London-Jersey 1853). Leroux is best known for his major work *De l'Humanité*,[10] where he set himself the task of synthesizing "the positive religions" into a single suprareligion of humanity. In that "great word," which accounted for all religions, he hoped to show that the cult of humanity is fueled by a cosmic vision of which the relationship of the subject to his shit is a necessary motor. The religion of humanity and the cult of *besoin* are mutually elucidated by their proximity in the work of this man who spent a good part of his militant life trying to convince his contemporaries that it was possible to abolish poverty completely—to fulfill everybody's needs—by asking each to make a contribution of his shit to the State.

It would be foolish not to recognize in this scheme the *literal* truth of State-idolatry, which keeps millions of subjects in check and yokes the "obscene and ferocious" discourse of the tyrannical State to that of the omnipotent Educator. Were it not for the master's iron rule, his subjects would smear one another with shit rather than make a gift of it.

Totalitarianism speaks thus: "Methodically collect your manure and give it to the State that wishes you well. Give up this shit, this fruit of your labor, and in return, I will fulfill all your needs and lavish you with such gifts that you shall lack for nothing." This law is framed as nature's own. Feudal and capitalist oppression always gave its subjects cause for lack, with the exception of a handful who were satiated at the expense of others. The State, on the other hand, delivers the subject from need and returns him to a state of nature. It is along these lines that Pierre Leroux developed his theory of the *circulus*, a theory specifically designed to refute Malthus (no doubt one of capitalism's most ignoble ideologues).

As is widely known, Malthus held that the population has a natural tendency to grow in inverse geometrical proportion to its resources, which in turn increase in arithmetic progression. This explained the disastrous impoverishment of his day, which, Malthus reasoned, would only worsen until "two centuries hence the proportionate relationship of population to resources shall be equal to 256 to 9 . . . [unless measures are taken to] . . . prevent the growth of capital from falling below population growth." Economists generally reacted to this cry of alarm by recommending the practice of so-called conjugal caution, while the phanerogamous mores of the phalanstery advocated sterilization.

Seeing man as equipped by nature to reproduce his own subsistence, Pierre Leroux proffered a different response: "[I]t has fallen to me," he writes in his *Letter to the States of Jersey*, "to oppose to the Law of Malthus the genuine Law of Nature. This true Law of Nature is what I have called, in reference to the economists' notion of circulation, a natural circle or *circulus*." It was certainly a

I'M WITH
SHAKSPEARE
[*sic*]

matter of a circle, since man was in a position to satisfy his needs by attending to them. "I have, therefore, proven," he continues,

F I G . 6 . 7

that nature has established a circle that is half production and half consumption; neither of these halves could exist without the other, and each is equal to the other;

This circle constitutes the physiological existence of each being, and even of each organ inside each being: Nutrition and Secretion. . . .

That these secretions really are, from the point-of-view of nature, the price of its subsistence, being destined to other beings in the same manner that the secretions of other beings are destined to it. . . .

I have proven:

That it is supremely iniquitous to blame nature for society's present ills, and to say as Malthus does, that "Nature, itself, condemns to death the man who does not have a place setting at the banquet of life," that is, the man whose services are, economically speaking, useless.

That the most impoverished proletarian who dies of hunger in our cities when he is denied the crumbs of that banquet does not starve through the fault of God, as that body that dies from hunger is an admirable laboratory, and a work of God so perfect that all the mighty of the earth together with all the men of science could not artificially produce the useful riches it produces.

But that this man, who had within him the right to live and the strength to do so, should die because the known circle of the economists, by excluding it from its necessary tie to the earth, has destroyed the natural circle.

130
·
131

"AND I FASHIONED EARTH"

To produce is literally to shit. "Do you in fact produce anything with all your riches?" Leroux demands of Malthus. "No, it is nature that produces everything, and when you get to the bottom of all your means of production, industry sends you back to agriculture, and in the end, to your manure."

Does not this immense toilet of a universe, with its "divine power of earthly silt from which the creator eternally fashions all beings," shed light on the fetish of physiocrats, so obsessed with earth and so skillful at hiding its impurities in their discursive maneuverings of commerce? At the very least, this sullied soil reconciles humanity's two Golden Ages—that of its origins and of its becoming—by vowing an end to wretchedness in reclaiming the means of creation for a world where the very notion of labor disappears.

On seeing a worker in the streets of London who had scrawled "worker seeking labor" on his shovel, Leroux protests that "every last one of these poor wretches could live off his own manure." He could not accept that "God could have created a being   I'M WITH SHAKSPEARE [*SIC*] who would have been incapable of self-sustenance by way of the usefulness of his secretions for other beings." Pierre Leroux's account of his wanderings through the streets of London—which should certainly be ranked with the most remarkable literary works of the day—is a litany of ills encountered in neighborhoods inhabited by every stripe of colonial immigrants. At one point, he interrupts his description to recall the words of God commanding the Prophet to make bread from human excrement; the moment, an epiphanic one for Leroux, leads him to reproduce the experiment of creation, to reenact the divine production of silt:

That day I resolved, therefore, to follow God's counsel. I went and purchased an old iron mortar that I had seen for sale in the Borough, and I carried it myself with some effort. I then went to the Vauxhall Bridge in search of a load of river sand from the Thames. I gave that sand many washings, so as to ensure it was free of dirt. I pounded it into as fine a dust as I could manage.

I then took charcoal which I pounded.

I took ashes from our hearth, that is to say ashes from coal. I took a brick and pounded it as well.

I mixed these substances to form a mineral-vegetal powder.

I mixed this powder to my urine and to my excrement and I fashioned earth.[11]

132
.
133

FIG. 6.9
We can appreciate the orthodoxy of this genesis in a variety of ways. Its insolent beauty dazzles us more than it makes us laugh, even when Pierre Leroux speaks of the "lovely pods" of the green beans he grew in this earth. The fable of a soil fertilized by man's seed and the sexually infantile theory of the *cloaca* are here fused in the form of an earth engendered by human waste. Leroux translates the most primitive of creation myths in which the earth gives birth to itself into the socialist ethos of *"pulvis es, et in pulverum reverteris"*—the dream of a world in which man, the microcosm of God, can ensure his subsistence through a daily defecation that reenacts divine creation.

TO EACH ACCORDING TO HIS *BESOINS*

Leroux's delirium proved as futile as any number of comparable utopian schemes. Although distinguished by its beauty, his plan is nonetheless part of the broader historical emergence of socialist thought. Leroux was not alone in placing shit at the heart of his dream of the universal gratification of human needs. Some of Fourier's disciples, for example, argued that the failure of the phalanstery was due to the shortage of manure. And Fourier, himself, in response to Mme. Bauder-Dulary's disappointment at the failed experiment on her lands, reportedly said: "Give me manure, Madam." From Bentham's injunction "never practice a *besoin* in pure loss" to the sweeping slogan "to each his own" (which still regulates the illusory destiny of many), there is a discursive continuity, a consistency regarding the historical mark of a relationship to shit in which excremental metaphors accumulate and retention is a condition of happiness. Shit is the precious object par excellence, the object that must not be squandered at any cost. But it is equally that which the subject must renounce, "religiously collect," and deliver to the State under a double burden: on one hand, the promise of an end to lack and, on the other, the threat of hardship, given a lack of discipline.

The aim is not to determine whether the object as such—or its substitutes—is of greater consequence to the social order. The search for primary causes is always inscribed in teleological discourses and the policies to which they give rise. The repugnant thing has been identified, in an argument hazarded against reason—insofar as reason is the mechanism of a State that continually refines its modes of oppression by barricading power behind

I'M WITH SHAKSPEARE [*SIC*]

political knowledge and primitive belief behind positivist technology. All that tumbles are a few masks; the sound we hear is not their fall—they are quickly retrieved—but the derisive laughter that pulls them down, the kind of laughter one encounters only in the theater or the circus.

FIG. 6.10 In this spirit, let us turn to the tried and true repertoire of spectacle and imagine ourselves at the Peking Opera or a performance of the Grand Guignol. First, remember that in Pierre Leroux's day the *niao* and the *fenn* were more precious than yellow gold. When people emerged from the Koun-tse-fan (a public bathroom in the shape of a hallway "lined by stalls in the fashion of the boxes in an opera house"), they did not leave a tip in the custodian's bowl. Rather, it was the custodian who distributed a *sapèque* to all comers in exchange for the shit that they left behind.[12] We must further recall that the theory of the *circulus* entails "relying on one's own powers" for social subsistence and reproduction, and that this slogan coincides with the figure of the "garbage man," that hero of the Cultural Revolution, Lei Feng. The stage is set with a placard displaying the following phrase from the unforgettable writings of Pierre Leroux: "I have had the experience of the Chinese. Truly, I have no need for chemists."[13]

Now, let the play begin. Our fable of bourgeois science's insidious resistance of proletarian science takes the form of an original dialogue by Pierre Leroux:[14]

Scholar: *Hey, don't you know that 1000 liters of urine contains 933 parts water?*

Self: *Well, yeah . . .*

Scholar: *And you think nothing of it?!*

Self: *What do you want me to think? It's not going to make me change my mind.*

Scholar: *But it's obvious. If you take 1000 liters of urine and subtract the water, you have 67 parts—various salts including uric acid. Say the average man pisses 730 liters of urine a year, the proportion would be 1000: 67 = 730: x, or x = $\frac{67 \times 730}{1000}$. In other words, around 49 liters of usable material. How is a man supposed to live on 49 liters of various salts plus a little uric acid?*

Self *(laughing): So that's how chemists see things!*

Scholar *(getting red under the collar): Don't be an idiot. Do you have any idea how many hectoliters of powdery stuff it takes to fertilize a hectare of land?*

Self: *Go ahead, tell me.*

Scholar: *Twenty, you need twenty. And don't try to deny that it takes at least one hectare of well-fertilized land to feed a man.*

I'M WITH
SHAKSPEARE
[SIC]

Self: *Sure, on average a hectare of farmland turns a profit of about 1,500 francs, which means 500 francs net. Okay, three quarters of the people in France live on a lot less than that. But given the current state of agriculture, it takes one hectare of good, well-fertilized land to feed a man—that is, to meet all his immediate needs.*

Scholar: *Well, where are you going to get fertilizer for that hectare? You need 20 hectoliters of powder and all you've got is 49 liters of urine and feces.*

Self: *If I looked at it your way of course I'd come up short.*

Scholar: *What other way is there to look at it?*

Self: *Now it's your turn to answer the questions. Don't you know how much water there is in milk?*

Scholar: *I can't remember.*

FIG. 6.11

Self: *Well, actually,* there's exactly as much water in milk as there is in urine. *Check out Berzèlius's study. A hundred parts skimmed cow's milk contains 92.875 parts water. The rest is made up of 2.600 parts casein, 3.500 parts milk sugars, 0.600 parts lactic acid and lactates, 0.185 soluble alkaline salts, and 0.230 parts phosphate of lime. Whole milk has a little less water, but not much: 87.6 parts per 100 liters. Do you want to know what's in mother's milk? According to M. Payen, for every 100 parts, there's 5.18 parts butter, 0.24 parts casein, 7.86 parts solid residue of evaporated buttermilk—and 85.80 parts water. You told me that every 1000 liters of urine contains 933 parts water, and I'm telling you that every 100 liters of milk contains 85 to 92 parts water. In other words, every 1000 parts contains 850 to 920 parts water. As you can see, milk has as much water as urine. If there is a difference, it's pretty minor. So, there's something similar about urine and milk that you failed to mention.*

136
•
137

Scholar: *What's your point?*

Self: *Now I have to ask you not to be an idiot. Milk contains large quantities of water and—still—you believe it's nourishing! You think that children and small animals grow on milk! Nonsense!*

Scholar: *I'm not sure what to say. It's true that milk contains as much water as urine; yet milk is nourishing and water is not.*

Self: *When you drink a glass of milk, you are consuming almost pure water, but you claim that milk nourishes.*

Scholar: *It's quite true. According to Berzèlius, when I have a glass of milk, I'm drinking 92 percent water.*

Self: *And, according to M. Payen, when your baby suckles at his mother's breast, he's imbibing 85 percent water. But he's growing up like a charm, your kid. And I, being particularly partial to Dr. Loudon's method, would advise his mother to keep nursing him until he's two or three years old. Eighty-five parts water, combined with the remaining fifteen parts, will give him blood, muscles, nerves, bones—in short, everything one needs to make a lovely boy.*

Scholar: *I have to admit Nature's chemistry is pretty remarkable.*

Self: *And your chemistry—or at least its scientific conclusions—are pretty stupid.*

Scholar: *And what do you mean by that?*

Self: *Isn't what we just said about milk also true of wine? Wine is pretty much made up of water.*

Scholar: *Pretty much.*

Self: *Here's an excellent bottle of Bordeaux. For every 100 liters, there are only 15 parts alcohol. Does that mean it's not wine, or that it won't get you drunk?*

Scholar: *No.*

Self: *Well, why is it that you haven't discovered that what's true of milk and wine might also be true of urine?*

Scholar: *Look, if you show me a creature who drinks urine like we drink milk or wine, and to whom it gives blood, muscles, nerves, and bones, I'll hold my peace.*

Self: *That's a precious admission, and it was wrested from you by the power of truth. Well, those beings exist.*

Scholar: *Show them to me.*

Self: *There is a book to be written—and I've been thinking about it for a long time, because I find our ignorance on the subject unbearable. But admit that if you never saw children gaining nourishment from milk or men growing reckless from wine, you wouldn't believe those things either. It's nothing but water, after all!*

Scholar: *You still haven't answered my objection about the powder.*

Self: *The powder has been made by chemists in keeping with their principles, by virtue of their ideas, and in accordance with their credo. In short, it's another absurdity.*

Scholar: *How can you not believe in chemistry?!*

Self: *I believe in Nature. As Shakspeare* [sic] *says: "There are more things in heaven and earth, Horatio, than are dreamt of in your philosophy." I'm with Shakspeare* [sic].

FIG. 6.12

I'M WITH
SHAKSPEARE
[SIC]

FIGURE 6. 2

Detail of Sir John Harrington's

flushed water lavatory

from *Metamorphosis of Ajax*, 1589.

Science Museum/Science & Society

Picture Library, London.

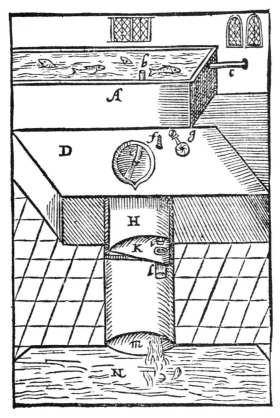

A. the Cesterne.
B. the little washer.
C. the wast pipe.
D. the seate boord.
E. the pipe that comes from the Cesterne.
F. the Screw.
G. the Scallop shell to cover it when it is shut downe.[53]
H. the stoole pot.
I. the stopple.
K. the current.
L. the sluce.[54]
M. N. the vault into which it falles: always remember that (   )[55] at noone and at night, emptie it and leave it halfe a foote deepe in fayre water. And this being well done, and orderly kept, your worst privie may be as sweet as your best chamber.

FIGURE 6.3
Walker Evans, *Store window, Brooklyn*, ca. 1931.
© Walker Evans Archive,
The Metropolitan Museum of Art, New York.

FIGURE 6.4
Manual training high school, Brooklyn, 1958.
New York City Board of Education Archives,
Milbank Memorial Library,
Teachers College, Columbia University.

FIGURE 6.5
Collection of the Municipal Archives of
the City of New York.

6.7. A spoonful of soil weighing 10 grams (dry) contains about 1.2 quintillion (1.2×10^{18}) exchange sites to which plant nutrients (Ca, K, etc.) may be held available for plant roots.

144
·
145

FIGURE 6.6

Mason White, Monument to Futurism, Como, Italy.

FIGURE 6.7

Soil Science Simplified, second edition,

Harpstead et al.,

Iowa University Press, Ames, Iowa, 1997.

FIGURE 6.8

Eugène Atget, *Terrain (Limoges)*, before 1900.

Albumen-silver print, $7 \times 9\frac{3}{8}$".

Abbott-Levy Collection. Partial gift of Shirley C. Burden,

The Museum of Modern Art, New York.

© 1999, The Museum of Modern Art, New York.

FIGURE 6.9

Pressure shower, 1889, from *Water Log:*

A Light Hearted Look at the Amenities of the Bathroom, 1975.

FIGURE 6.10

Hiroshi Sugimoto, *5th Avenue Theater*, 1997.

Courtesy The Sonnabend Gallery, New York.

FIGURE 6.11

Washington D.C. water supply.

Courtesy The Library of Congress, Washington, D.C.

FIGURE 6.12

"Coining," *Encyclopédie, ou Dictionnaire raisonné des sciences,*

des arts et des metiers, par une société de gens de lettres,

Diderot and D'Alembert, 1779–1782.

Bibliothèque Nationale, Paris.

notes

INTRODUCTION

1 · See Renée Balibar and Dominique Laporte, *Le Français national: politique et pratiques de la langue nationale sous la Revolution Française*, introduction by Etienne Balibar and Pierre Macherey (Paris: Hachette, 1974).

2 · In the late 1970s, Laporte was heavily involved with the psychoanalytic journal *Ornicar?* and its intellectual circle, whose prominent members included Jacques Lacan and Jean-Claude Milner.

3 · Parody, for instance, is evident in the title, which pokes fun at "The History of You-Name-It" fad of the Annales school.

4 · Sigmund Freud, *Civilization and Its Discontents*, trans. James Strachey (New York: Norton, 1961), pp. 51–52.

5 · See Jean-Louis Flandrin, *Familles, parenté, maison, sexualité dans l'ancienne société* (Paris: Hachette, 1976), pp. 97–100.

6 · See Alain Corbin, *The Foul and the Fragrant: Odor and the French Social Imagination*, trans. Miriam Kochan (Cambridge, MA: Harvard University Press, 1984).

7 · See Fortier, *La politique de l'espace Parisien* (Paris: C.O.R.D.A., 1975); Michel Foucault, ed. *Les Machines à guérir* (Brussels: Madraga, 1979); Anthony Vidler, *The Writing of the Walls: Architectural Theory in the Late Enlightenment* (New York: Princeton Architectural Press, 1987).

8 · Le Roy, *Précis d'un ouvrage sur les hopitaux* (1777) quoted in Vidler, *The Writings of the Walls*, p. 61.

9 · The urban cemetery brought the dead and the living into intolerable proximity, a perverse juxtaposition that epitomized the consistent promiscuity of city space: the cesspool in the street, the slaughterhouse in the residential neighborhood. Spaces of confinement such as prisons and hospitals, on the other hand, epitomized another form of urban pathology: density. Metaphorically, the prison substituted for the city when it came to issues of overcrowding. Together, the spatial transformation of prison and cemetery set the tone for the redefinition of the norms of urban space in the late Enlightenment: decongestion, disconnection, separation, and isolation are the imperatives of its reorganization.

CHAPTER 1

1 · De Seyssel, *Prologue à la traduction de Justin*, cited by Ferdinand Brunot, *Histoire de la langue française des origines à nos jours*, vol. 2 (Paris: A. Colin, 1966–1978), pp. 29–30. See also Ferdinand Brunot, "Un projet d'enricher, magnifier, et sublimer la langue francaise en 1509," *Revue d'Histoire Littéraire*, 1, p. 27.

2 · Grégoire, "Rapport sur la nécessité et les moyens d'anéantir les patois et d'universaliser l'usage de la langue française," *National Convention, Session of The Sixteenth Prairial, Year 2* (May 1794).

3 · Author's emphasis.

4 · [Joachim du Bellay, French poet and theorist of language, belonged to an important group of writers active in Lyon in the sixteenth century. Following the example of Petrarch, the group employed striking metaphors and the sonnet form. Du Bellay himself was one of the first to approach the French language scientifically, as though it were a subject of natural history.—Tr.]

5 · *Uns bleibt ein Erdenrest*
zu tragen peinlich,
und wär' er von Asbest,
er ist nicht reinlich.

Earth remnants molest us,
To bear them is toil,
Were they asbestos
They still would soil.
(Johann Wolfgang Goethe, Faust, trans. Walter Arndt. New York: W. W.
Norton & Co., 1976, p. 303, lines 11, 954—11, 957).

These lines are cited by Freud in the preface to *Der Unratt in Sitte, Brauch, Glauben und Gewohnheistrecht der Völker,* the German translation of John G. Bourke, *Scatological Rites of All Nations* (Washington D.C.: W. H. Lowdermilk & Co., 1891).

6 · Roland Barthes, *Sade, Fourier, Loyola* (Paris: Editions du Seuil, 1971), p. 140.

7 · Saint Augustine, *De magistro* I, "De Locutionis Significatione," cited by Jacques Lacan in "Séminaire I," *Le Séminaire de Jacques Lacan,* ed. Jacques-Alain Miller (Paris: Seuil, 1973).

8 · See Gérard Wajeman, "Odor di Femina," *Ornicar?* no. 7. [The French *parfum* (perfume) can be parsed to read *pare/fumier* or counter/manure.—Tr.]

9 · Vaugelas, *Remarques sur la langue française,* 1674 edition, p. 593.

10 · Freud, *Civilization and Its Discontents,* chaps. 3 and 4.

11 · Among the many testimonies attesting to the shortage of facilities and ensuing discomfort, we select the following extravagant missive written on October 9, 1694 by Madame la duchesse d'Orléans:

Fontainbleau, October 9, 1694

To the Electress of Hanover,

> *You are indeed fortunate to shit whenever you may please and to do so to your heart's content! . . . We are not so lucky here. I have to hold on to my turd un-*

til evening; the houses next to the forest are not equipped with facilities. I have the
misfortune of inhabiting one and consequently the displeasure of having to shit
outside, which gravely perturbs me because I like to shit at my ease with my ass
fully bared. Item all manner of people can see us shitting; there are men who walk
by, women, girls, boys, abbeys, Swiss Guards. . . . As you can see, there is no plea-
sure without pain, and if we did not have to shit, I would be happy as a fish in
water here at Fontainbleau. (Correspondence of Madame la duchess d'Orléans,
Princesse palatine. Paris, Charpentier, 1855, vol. II, p. 385)

12 · Cf. Pierre Legendre, *Jouir du pouvoir, Traité de la bureaucratie patriote*
(Paris: Editions de Minuit: col. Critique, 1976).

13 · Cf. F. Liger, "Fosses d'aisances, latrines, urinoirs et vidanges," vol. I,
no. 8, in *Dictionnaire historique et pratique de la voirie, de la construction, de la*
police municipale et de la contituité, Paris, 1875. A goldmine of erudition and
indispensible complement to *Biblioteca scatologica* of Jannet, Payen and
Veinant, Paris, 1849.

14 · For a tribute to the *cloaca maxima,* see H. du Roselle, *Les eaux, les égouts*
et les fosses d'asiances dans leurs rapports avec les épidémies, Amiens, 1867.

15 · Christopher Columbus, "Letter from Jamaica," 1503, cited by Karl
Marx in *Capital: A Critique of Political Economy,* trans. Ben Fowkes (New
York: Penguin Books in association with New Left Review, 1990), Book I,
chap. 3.

16 · On the alchemical dimension of circulation, see Marx, op. cit., Book I.
The equivalence of language and currency persists verbatim in the Nation-
alist discourse. See, for example, the informative article by Michel Debré,
"La langue française et la science universelle," in *La Recherche,* no. 72, November 1976.

17 · Joachim du Bellay, *La Deffence et illustration de la langue française,* fac-
similie of the original edition of 1549 (Geneva: Droz, 1949).

18 · See Pierre Legendre, op. cit., esp. pp. 131–146.

19 · On the sources of this *détournement*, see, for the "beastly insanity," Phillipe Sollers, *H: roman* (Paris: Editions du Seuil, 1973). [In this passage, Laporte is paraphrasing and riffing on Mallarmé's "Aboli bibelot d'inanité sonore."—Tr.]

20 · Shakespeare, *Timon of Athens*, cited by Marx, op. cit., Book I.

CHAPTER 2

1 · According to Elie Reclus, *Les Primitifs*, Paris, 1885, as cited by John G. Bourke, op. cit.

2 · Author's emphasis.

3 · Cited in F. Liger, "Fosses d'aisances, latrines, urinoirs et vidanges," in *Dictionnaire historique et pratique de la voirie, de la construction, de la police municipale et de la continuité*, vol. 1, Paris, 1875.

4 · Cited in Paulet, *Engrais humains*, p. 285.

5 · Cf. Pliny, *Natural History*, Book XXVII: "The authors unanimously agree that human excretions are the best possible fertilizers."

6 · According to F. Liger, op. cit., who draws his sources from Cato and Varo, stercoration was not widely practiced in the Roman Republic.

7 · According to F. Liger, op. cit.

8 · [*Model latrines, built under a pigeon coop and ventilated by means of pigeon heat and serving for the preparation of fertilizer.*—Tr.]

9 · Cato, *De Re Rustica*, Books II and XV.

10 · According to the *Géoponiques*, the redemption by means of water was practiced by the peoples of Arabia: "When they have sufficiently dried it,

they dip it in water and dry it a second time, and say that in this way waste is very beneficial to the grapevine."

11 · Gryphius, *In latrinis mortui et occisi*, 1593, in-no.8, as cited in the *Bibliotheca scatologica*, Paris, 1849.

12 · Cf. Georges Bataille, preface to *La Sorcière*, and Roland Barthes, *Michelet* (Paris: Ecrivains de toujours, 1954).

13 · See Roland Barthes, *Sade, Fourier, Loyola.*

14 · See especially Jean-Louis Flandrin, *Families in Fomer Times: Kinship, Household, and Sexuality*, trans. Richard Southern (New York: Cambridge University Press, 1979).

15 · ". . . si l'ordure qui dore dans les champs fait or qui dure dans les allées citadines, l'odeur de l'ordure dure où l'or dort."

16 · [Laporte is referring to the exposed infrastructure of Beaubourg, Musée National d'Art Contemporain, Centre Georges Pompidou, and the lengthy excavation and transformation of the adjacent marketplace, Les Halles, into a modern shopping mall in the 1970s and '8os.—Tr.]

17 · See Pierre Legendre, op. cit., particularly the chapter "L'Etat pur."

18 · Expression borrowed from Jacques Lacan.

19 · See Legendre, op. cit.

20 · *Les dix livres d'Architecture de Vitruve, corrigés et traduits par M. Perrault*, 2nd edition, Book XV, chap. 10, note 6, Paris, 1684.

21 · [In French, *le privé* designates both "the private realm" and "watercloset." This ambiguity is fully exploited by Laporte in his conflation of the private space and the space of excrement. We have thus retained the French word *privé* whenever this rhetorical ambiguity was instrumental to his argument.—Tr.]

22 · See Molière, *L'Etourdi ou le contre-temps*, 1658, act 3, scene 13.

23 · Scarron, *Japhet d'Arménie*, cited in P. Larousse, *Dictionnaire du XIXe siècle*, "Fosses d'aisances."

24 · Louis Sébastian Mercier, *Tableau de Paris*, vol. V, chap. 350, Amsterdam, 1782–1789. [Here the equation between the "shovel of the garbage collector" and the "foul language of the street" confirms a homology between the politics of language and the politics of shit.—Tr.]

CHAPTER 3

1 · "Conférences aux Amériques," *Scilicet*, no. 6/7.

2 · Jules Ferry, who is the most splendid example dedicated to the State (his colonial bugle still resonates in the ears of the veterans of the communale), certainly was touching on something when, in writing "Les Comptes d'Haussman," he stirred up the shit of the Statesman who was the *Grand Collecteur* par excellence.

3 · James Joyce, *Ulysses* (New York: Vintage Books, 1961), p. 131.

4 · See Jonathan Swift, *The grand mystery, or art of meditating over an house of office, restor'd and unveil'd; after the manner of the ingenious Dr. S——ft [Swift]. With observations historical, political and moral; on the dignity, usefulness, and pleasantness of that study. With several new improvements, and proposals for better accommodating the nobility and gentry, of both sexes, in their natural necessities, and for making London the most magnificent city in the world. Dedicated to the profound Dr. W——[Wotton], followed by Proposal for erecting and maintaining publick offices of ease within the cities and suburbs of London and Westminster*, London: Printed for A. More, near St. Paul's, and sold by the booksellers of London and Westminster, 1726.

5 · Cf. Juvenal, Sat. VI, *Des Femmes:* Noctibus hic ponunt lecticas micturiunt hic Effigiensque deae longis siphonibus implent; Inque vices equitant,

ac, luna teste, moventur Inde domos abeunt: tu calcas, luce reverse, Conjugis urinam, magnos, visurus amicos.

6 · Swift, op. cit., pp. 20–21.

7 · Ibid., pp. 5–6.

8 · *New Testament*, Ps. 113.

9 · [The French for "to smell" is *sentir*, the same word as "to feel."—Tr.]

10 · Cf. Ph. Ariès, *L'Enfant et la vie familiale sous l'Ancien Régime* (Paris: Seuil, 1973), p. 392.

11 · Cf. Dominque Colas, "Lénine tayloriste," *Critique*, no. 358, March 1977.

12 · Pierre Guyotat, "La découverte de la logique," in *Cahiers du Chemin*, January 1977.

13 · [Here, Laporte is referring to Molière's *L'Avare* (*The Miser*) and Balzac's *La Comédie Humaine* (*The Human Comedy*), whose portrayals of avarice in the characters of Harpagon and Gobseck respectively have long been part of the French literary canon.—Tr.]

14 · See especially *Arrêt du parlement du 13 septembre 1533*, Article 2. "They (the cart drivers) will load all muds and offals. The bourgeois will only be held to cleaning." This was confirmed by the Ruling of 1563, previously cited.

CHAPTER 4

1 · Suetonius, *Vespasien*, Book XXIII: "Reprehendenti filio Tito, quod etiam urinae vectigal commentus esset, pecuniam ex prima pensione admovit ad nares, sciscitans: "Nunc odore offedretur: et illo negante, atqui, e lotio est."

2 · Balzac, *Sarassine*, as cited in Roland Barthes, *S/Z*, trans. Richard Miller (New York: Hill and Wang, 1974), p. 39.

3 · Cf. Foucault, *Histoire de la sexualité*, vol. 1, "La Volonté de savoir" (Paris: Gallimard, 1976).

4 · Cf. Dr. Cornay, *Rapport*, of November 16, 1853 and A. Sponi, *De la vidange, au passé, au présent at au futur*, Report to the magistrates in charge of the administration of the city of Paris, Paris, 1856, vol. I, in-8th.

5 · Ibid.

6 · *Maison de Marie-Claire*, March 1977, p. 100.

7 · Gaston Bachelard, *La Formation de l'esprit scientifique; contribution à une psychanalyse de la connaissance objective* (Paris: J. Vrin, 1947), p. 169.

8 · Foucault, "La Volonté de savoir," p. 194.

9 · Condillac, *Traité des Sensations* in *Dessein de cet ouvrage*, 1798.

10 · Ibid., I, 1, *Des premières connaissances d'un homme borné au sens de l'odorat*.

11 · Immanuel Kant, *Critique of Judgement*, trans. J. H. Bernard (New York: Hafner Press, 1951), p. 50. Author's emphasis. The ensuing discussion that centers on Kant developed in the aftermath of a question raised by Alain Grosrichard with regard to my paper, "Contribution pour une histoire de la merde: la merde des asiles, 1830–1880," published in *Analytica*, no. 4, July 1977.

12 · Kant, ibid., pp. 38–41.

13 · Kant, *Observations sur le sentiment du beau et du sublime* (Paris: Vrin, 1969), p. 44.

14 · Ibid.

15 · Freud, op. cit., p. 46.

16 · Kant, *Observations sur le sentiment du beau et du sublime*, p. 42.

17 · Cf. Kant, op. cit., pp. 60, 82 (note 34 by Roger Kempf).

18 · Kant, *Critique of Judgement*, p. 195.

CHAPTER 5

1 · [During the second century B.C., Cato the Elder and Columella both wrote on agriculture in all its manifestations. Cato's work in particular voices the traditional Roman attitude that simplicity and industry are the essence of country life and the base of moral character.—Tr.]

2 · [These figures, with the exception of the lyric poet Catullus, are all notable for the encyclopedic range of their works. Dioscurides was the author of a much-consulted handbook on the treatment of ailments and the making of medecine. Apuleius wrote a cookbook for the preparation of imperial banquets. Strabo discussed the geography of the entire known world, complete with investigation of flora, fauna, and custom, and Diodores of Sicily assembled a monumental compilation of Greek mythology. Pliny the Elder worked from some of these sources to write his vast encyclopedia on every aspect of the natural world, *The Natural History*, composed in the first century A.D.—Tr.]

3 · Cf. Cato, *De Re Rustica*, Book CLVII.

4 · Pliny, *The Natural History*, Book XXVIII, XIX, trans. W. H. S. Jones (Loeb Classic Library, Cambridge: Harvard University Press and London: William Heinemann, Ltd., 1963), pp. 47–51.

5 · "Fresh droppings from cows who have fed on grasses effectively soothe inflammations, wounds and tumors. . . . As the temperament of the male and the female are different, we cannot discount that the droppings of a bull will differ in a certain measure from those of a cow. . . . Bull droppings are particularly successful for returning a wandering womb to its place." Malouin, *Chimie médicinale*, 2 vol., 2nd ed., Paris, 1755, Book I, p. 122. Cited by Bachelard in *La Formation de l'Esprit scientifique*, p. 179.

6 · Testimonial.

7 · Pliny, *Natural History*, Books XXX and XV.

8 · Ibid., Books XXX and II.

9 · F. Liger, op. cit.

10 · *Nouveau Larousse Illustré*.

11 · *Suite de la matière médicale de M. Geoffroy*, by Arnault de Nobleville Salerne. Règne animal, Book VI. Cinquième et dernière classe: des Quadrupèdes, Paris, 1757, pp. 468–476. An excerpt was published in the *Journal de Médecine de Paris*, February 19, 1905.

12 · Cf. Macquer, de l'Acadénue Royal de Science, *Eléments de Chymie pratique*, 3 vols., Paris, 1751, Book II, p. 406, cited by Bachelard, op. cit., p. 180.

13 · Geoffroy, op. cit., p. 474.

14 · Barthes, *Sade, Fourier, Loyola*, p. 131.

15 · Ibid., p.148.

16 · O'Donovan, *Three Fragments of Irish Annals*, Dublin, 1860, cited in *Fragmentary Annals of Ireland*, Joan Newlon Radner (Dublin: Dublin Institute for Advanced Studies, 1978), p. 7. This fragment was translated into

French and published in the May 5, 1888 edition of *Mélusine*, a journal founded in 1875 in Paris by E. Rolland and A. Gaidoz, in an issue dedicated to myths, old traditions, and popular literature, etc. Bourke also cites it in *Scatalogic Rites of all Nations*, pp. 58–59.

17 · Cf. J. G. Bourke, op. cit., p. 59: "The bodies of Indian chiefs in Venezuela were incinerated, the ashes drunk in native liquor." (*Tuestanlo, muelenlo, y echado en vino lo beben y esto es gran houra.*) Gomara, *Historia de las Indias*, p. 203.

18 · Cf. *Mélusine*, May 1888.

19 · Op. Cit. Emphasis in original text.

20 · *Mélusine*, May, 1888, cited by Bourke, op. cit., chapter 9.

CHAPTER 6

1 · Cited by J. A. Miller, "La Machine panoptique de Jeremy Bentham," *Ornicar?* no. 3, 1975.

2 · [That is, utopian socialism, classical political economy, and Hegelian dialectics.—Tr.]

3 · Dr. E. L. Bertherand, *Mémoire sur la vidange des latrines et des urinoirs publics au point de vue hygiènique, agricole et commercial*, Lille, 1858. (Excerpt from the Archives de l'Agriculture du Nord, Book VI.)

4 · Ibid. Emphasis in original text.

5 · M. A. Chevallier, "Sur les urines, les moyens de les recueillir et de les utiliser," *Annales d'hygiène publique et de médecine légale*, January 1852, p. 68ff.

6 · Op. cit.

7 · Cf. Bertherand, op. cit. The process of pumps does not allow "like the old process, for the discovery of objects, articles of clothing, dead foetuses, organs, organic waste, etc. that can follow from the perpetration of a crime or other wrong-doing."

8 · A. Sponi, op. cit., pp. 14–15.

9 · A formula I borrow from François Walh, "Chute" in *Tel Quel*, no. 63, 1975.

10 · *De l'Humanité, de son principe et de son avenir, où se trouve exposée la vraie définition de la religion et où on explique le sens, la suite et l'enchainement du mosaïsme et du christianisme*, Paris, 1840, 2 vols., in-8th.

11 · In the appendix to the *Letter to the States of Jersey*, pp. 109–114, we note a passage that reads (p. 23), "I fashioned that which forms the basis for all the riches of the world, I fashioned *earth.*" Cf. appendix, p. 121: "Whereas I, I am so persuaded that the precise composition had yielded *earth*, that for me *all earth was that earth.*"

12 · Dr. Yvan, *Les Vespasiennes chinoises ou supériorité des agriculteurs chinois sur ceux d'Europe*, in *La Feuille de Village*, nos. 1, 2, and 7 of 1849.

13 · Appendix to *Letter to the States of Jersey*, op. cit., p. 178.

14 · Ibid., pp. 138–141.

HISTORY OF SHIT

DOMINIQUE LAPORTE

translated by Nadia Benabid and

Rodolphe el-Khoury

•

Written in Paris after the heady days of student revolt in May 1968 and before the
devastation of the AIDS epidemic, *History of Shit* is emblematic of a wild and adven-
turous strain of 1970s' theoretical writing that attempted to marry theory, politics,
sexuality, pleasure, experimentation, and humor. Radically redefining dialectical
thought and post-Marxist politics, it takes an important—and irreverent—position
alongside the works of such postmodern thinkers as Foucault, Deleuze, Guattari,
and Lyotard.

Laporte's eccentric style and ironic sensibility combine in an inquiry that is
provocative, humorous, and intellectually exhilarating. Debunking all humanist
mythology about the grandeur of civilization, *History of Shit* suggests instead that the
management of human waste is crucial to our identities as modern individuals—
including the organization of the city, the rise of the nation-state, the development
of capitalism, and the mandate for clean and proper language. Far from rising above
the muck, Laporte argues, we are thoroughly mired in it, particularly when we
appear our most clean and hygienic.

Laporte's style of writing is itself an attack on our desire for "clean language."
Littered with lengthy quotations and obscure allusions, and adamantly refusing to
follow a linear argument, *History of Shit* breaks the rules and challenges the conven-
tions of "proper" academic discourse.

Dominique Laporte, who died in 1984 at the age of thirty-five, was a psychoanalyst
and the coauthor of *Français national: politique et practiques de la langue nationale sous
la Révolution Française.*